EASY GUITAR
WITH NOTES & TAB

HALLOWEEN GUITAR SONGS

skac

ISBN 978-1-4950-2828-1

HAL•LEONARD®
CORPORATION
7777 W. BLUEMOUND RD. P.O. BOX 13819 MILWAUKEE, WI 53213

For all works contained herein:
Unauthorized copying, arranging, adapting, recording, Internet posting, public performance,
or other distribution of the printed music in this publication is an infringement of copyright.
Infringers are liable under the law.

Visit Hal Leonard Online at
www.halleonard.com

Abracadabra

Words and Music by Steve Miller

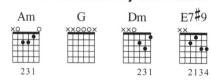

Strum Pattern: 1
Pick Pattern: 1

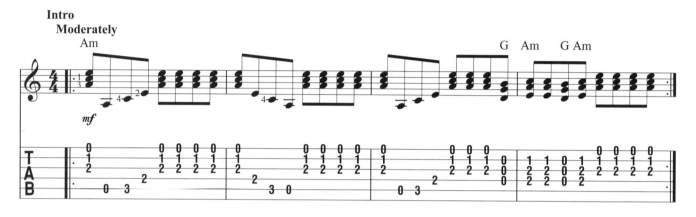

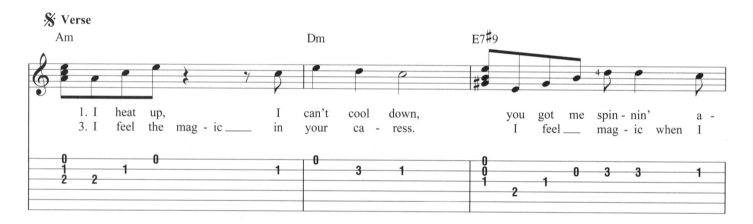

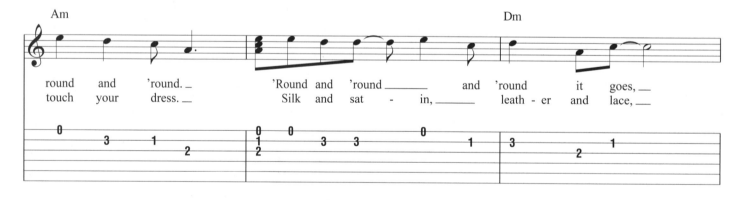

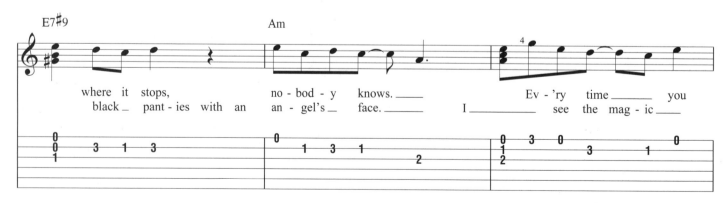

Copyright © 1982 by Sailor Music
All Rights Reserved   Used by Permission

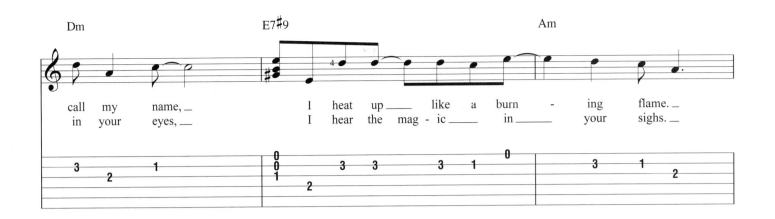

call my name, — .... I heat up ___ like a burn - ing flame. —
in your eyes, — .... I hear the mag - ic ___ in ___ your sighs. —

Burn - in' flame, ___ .... full of de - sire, ___ .... kiss me, ba - by, let the
Just when I think I'm gon - na get a - way, ___ .... I hear those words ___ that

Chorus

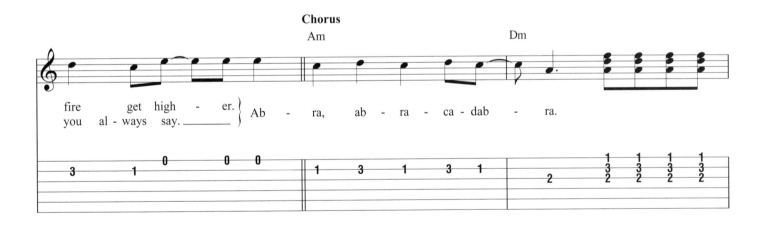

fire get high - er. } Ab - ra, ab - ra - ca - dab - ra.
you al - ways say.

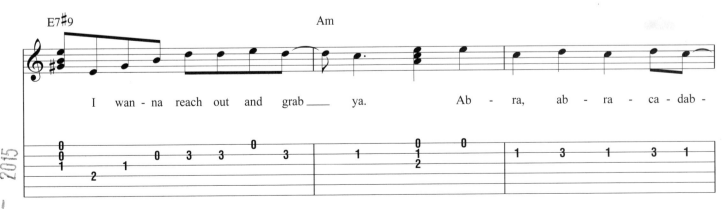

I wan - na reach out and grab ___ ya. .... Ab - ra, ab - ra - ca - dab -

BL - 2015

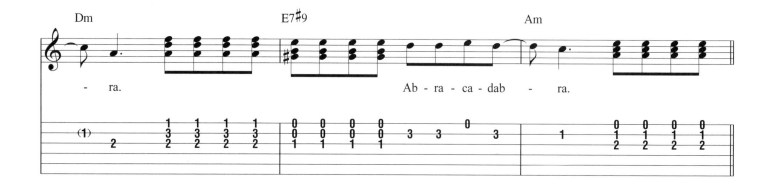

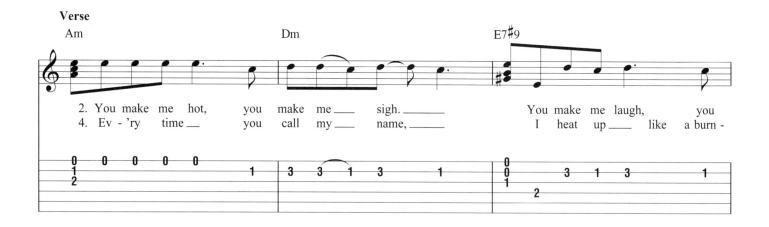

To Coda ⊕

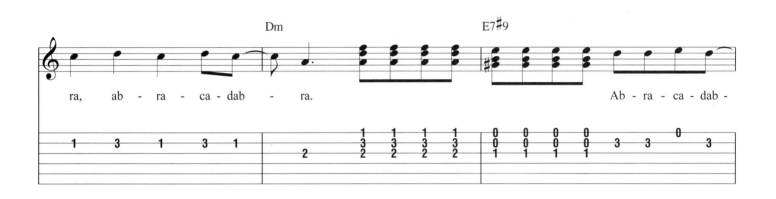

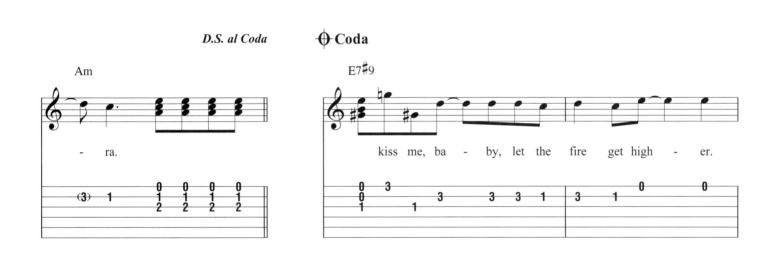

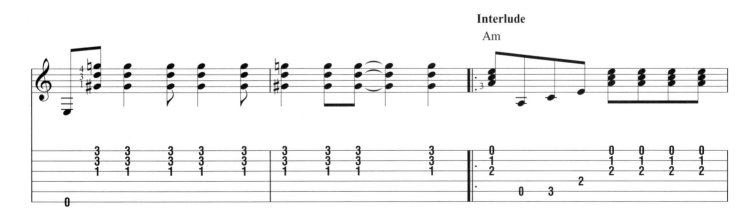

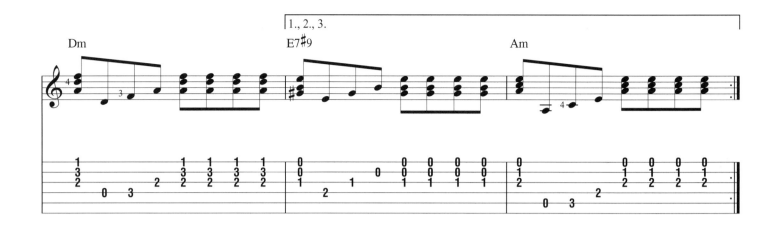

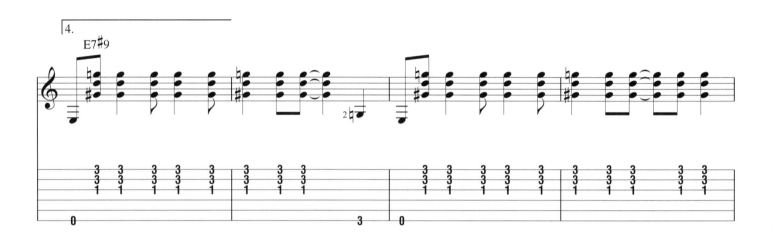

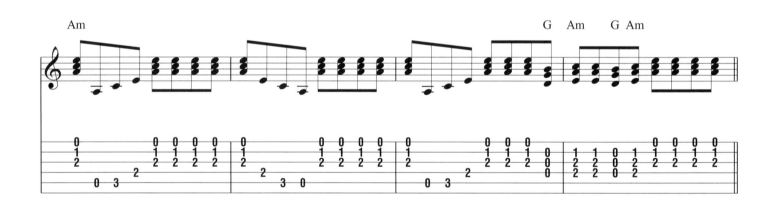

Outro

Repeat and fade

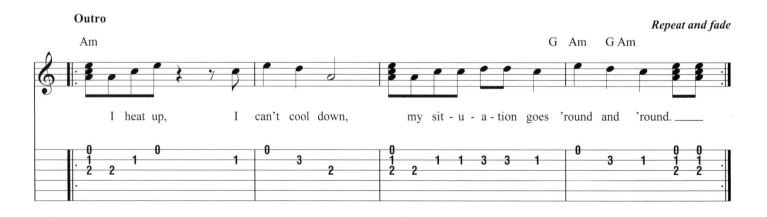

I heat up, I can't cool down, my sit - u - a - tion goes 'round and 'round. _____

Addams Family Theme

Theme from the TV Show and Movie
Music and Lyrics by Vic Mizzy

Additional Lyrics

2. Their house is a museum,
   Where people come to see 'um.
   They're really are a screem,
   The Addams Family.

3. So get a witches shawl on,
   A broom stick you can crawl on.
   We're gonna pay a call on,
   The Addams Family.

Copyright © 1964, Renewed 1992 by Unison Music Company
Administered by Next Decade Entertainment, Inc.
International Copyright Secured All Rights Reserved

Bad Moon Rising

Words and Music by John Fogerty

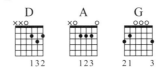

Strum Pattern: 4, 5
Pick Pattern: 1

Intro
Moderately fast

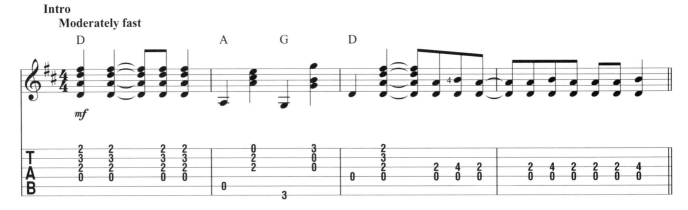

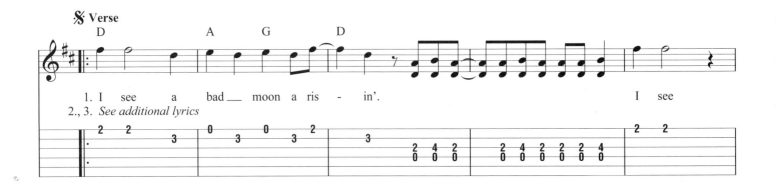

1. I see a bad ___ moon a ris - in'.   I see

2., 3. *See additional lyrics*

trou - ble on the way. ___   I see earth - quakes and light -

Copyright © 1969 Jondora Music
Copyright Renewed
International Copyright Secured   All Rights Reserved

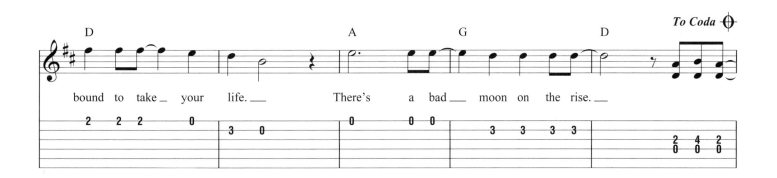

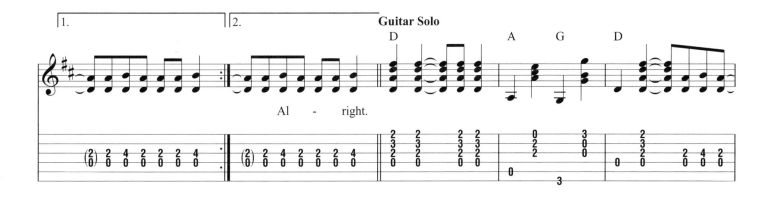

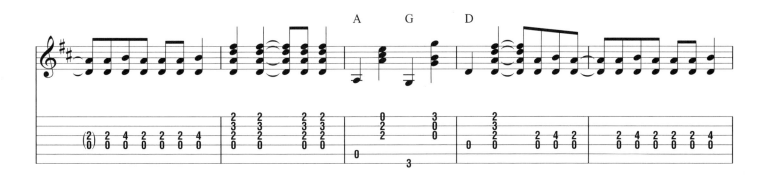

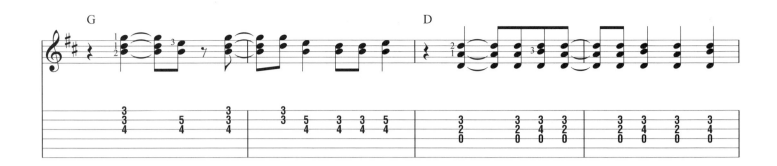

D.S. al Coda

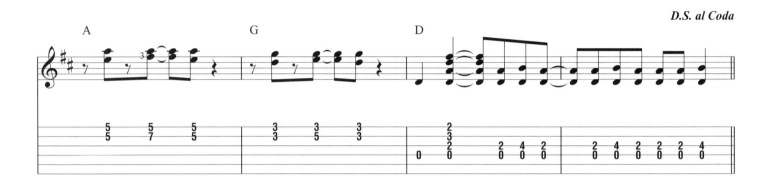

⊕ **Coda**

Outro-Chorus

Don't go a-round to-night. _____ Well, it's bound to take _ your

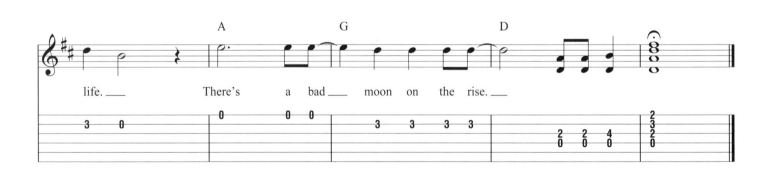

life. ___ There's a bad ___ moon on the rise. ___

Additional Lyrics

2. I hear hurricanes a blowin'.
   I know the end is comin' soon.
   I fear rivers overflowin'.
   I hear the voice of rage and ruin.

3. Hope you got your things together.
   Hope you are quite prepared to die.
   Looks like we're in for nasty weather.
   One eye is taken for an eye.

Bad Things

Theme from the HBO Series TRUE BLOOD
Words and Music by Jace Everett

© 2005 EMI BLACKWOOD MUSIC INC. and JACKABOY SONGS
All Rights Controlled and Administered by EMI BLACKWOOD MUSIC INC.
All Rights Reserved   International Copyright Secured   Used by Permission

Chorus

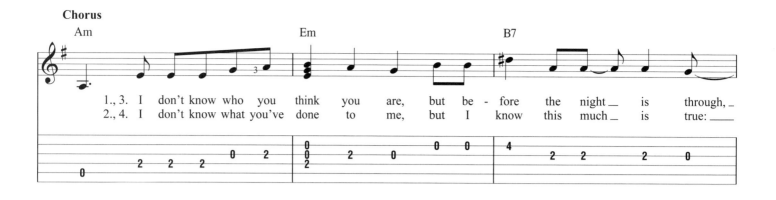

1., 3. I don't know who you think you are, but be - fore the night __ is through, __
2., 4. I don't know what you've done to me, but I know this much __ is true: ____

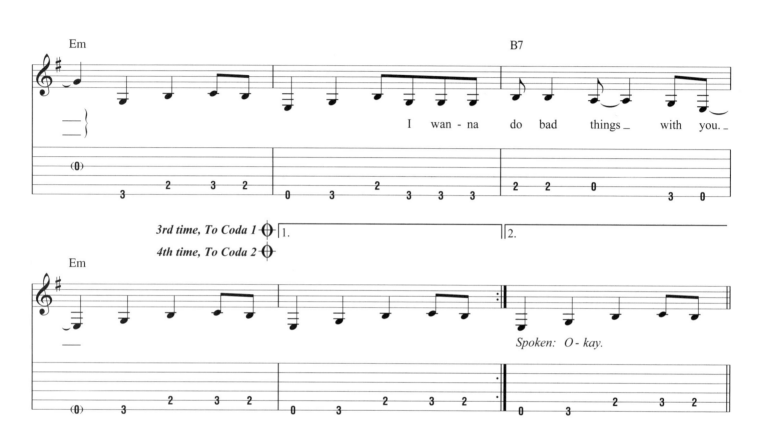

I wan - na do bad things __ with you. __

3rd time, To Coda 1 ⊕ [1.   [2.
4th time, To Coda 2 ⊕

Spoken: O - kay.

Guitar Solo

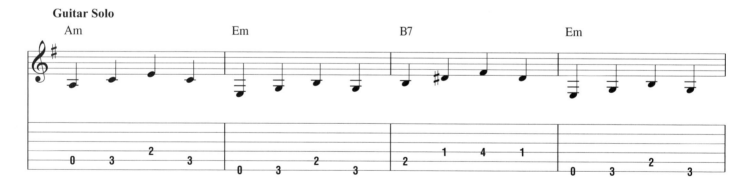

D.S. al Coda 1

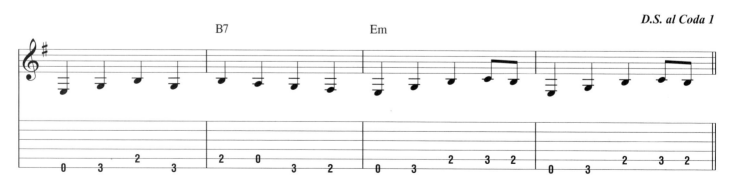

Coda 1

I wan-na do real ___

D.S. al Coda 2

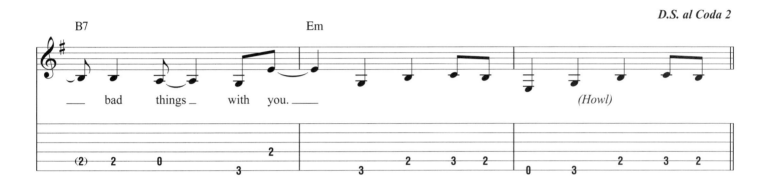

B7   Em

___ bad things ___ with you. ___   *(Howl)*

Coda 2

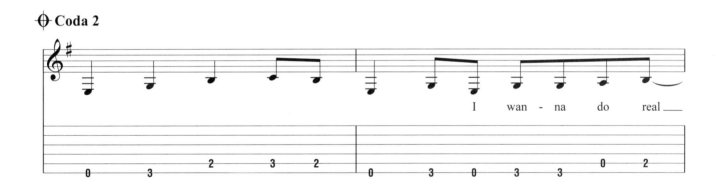

I wan-na do real ___

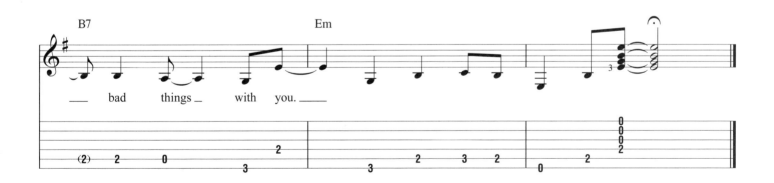

B7   Em

___ bad things ___ with you. ___

Additional Lyrics

Spoken: 3. *When you came in, the air went out.*
And all those shadows there filled up with doubt.

Creep

Words and Music by Albert Hammond, Mike Hazlewood, Thomas Yorke, Jonathan Greenwood, Colin Greenwood, Edward O'Brien and Philip Selway

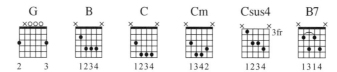

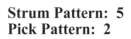

Strum Pattern: 5
Pick Pattern: 2

Intro
Moderately

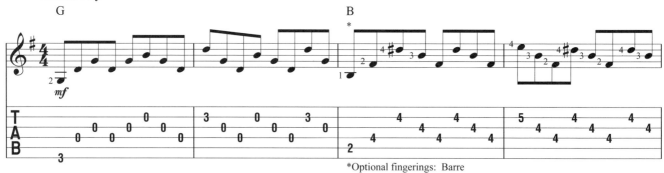

*Optional fingerings: Barre
3rd finger across 4th fret.

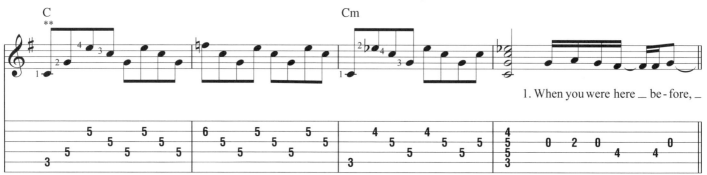

1. When you were here _ be-fore, _

**As before: 5th fret

Verse

3. *See additional lyrics*

could-n't look you in the eye. ___

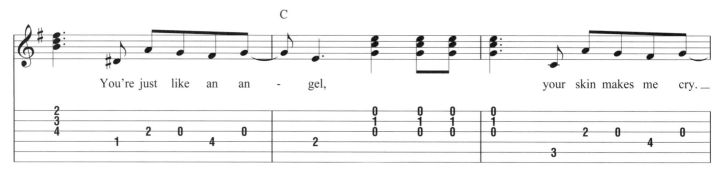

You're just like an an - gel, your skin makes me cry. _

© 1992 EMI APRIL MUSIC INC. and WARNER/CHAPPELL MUSIC LTD.
All Rights for WARNER/CHAPPELL MUSIC LTD. in the U.S. and Canada Administered by WB MUSIC CORP.
All Rights Reserved   International Copyright Secured   Used by Permission
- contains elements of "The Air That I Breathe" by Albert Hammond and Mike Hazlewood, © 1972 EMI APRIL MUSIC INC.

2. You float like a feath - er, ____
4., 5. *See additional lyrics*

in a beau - ti - ful world. __   I wish I were spe -

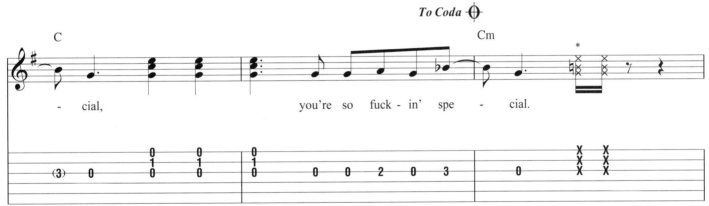

- cial,   you're so fuck - in' spe - cial.

*Muffled strings: Lay the fret hand across the strings with- out depressing and strike them w/ the pick hand.

Chorus

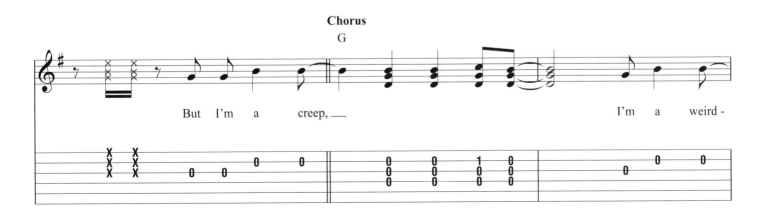

But I'm a   creep, __   I'm a weird -

What the hell __ am I do - ing here? __

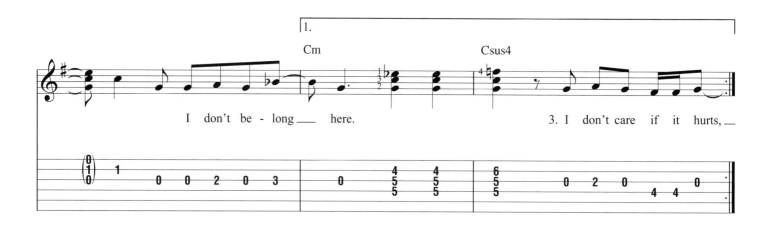

I don't be - long __ here.

3. I don't care if it hurts, __

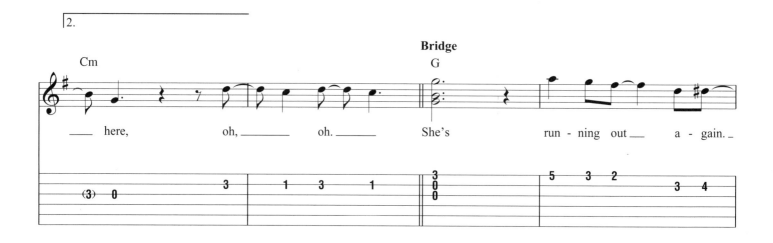

__ here, oh, __ oh. __ She's run - ning out __ a - gain. __

Bridge

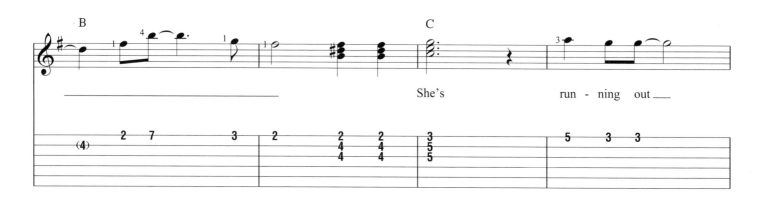

She's run - ning out __

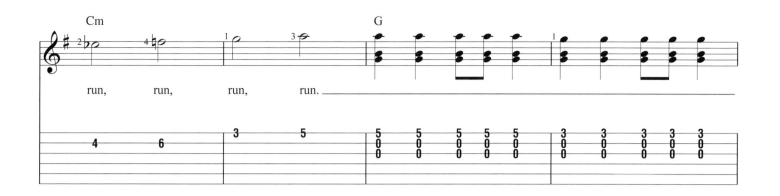

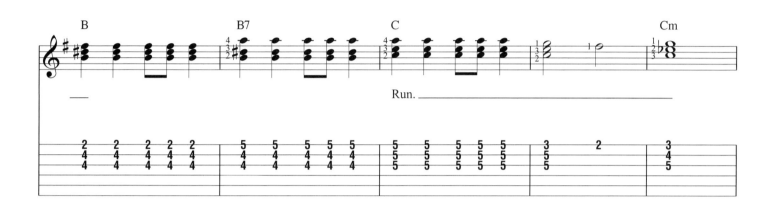

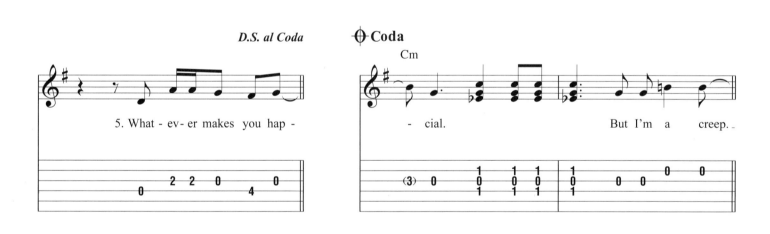

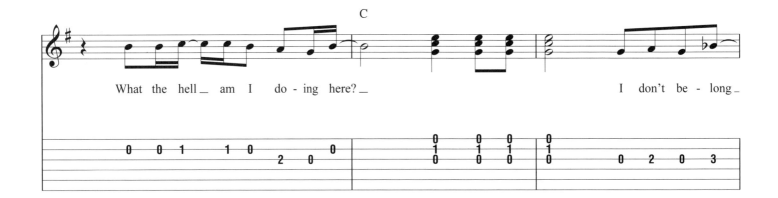

What the hell ___ am I do - ing here? ___   I don't be - long ___

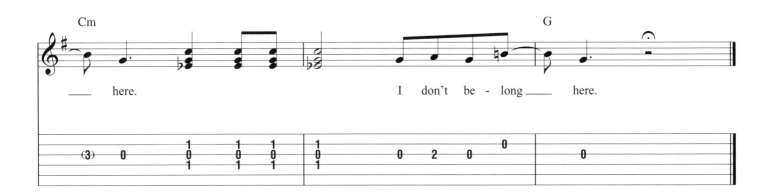

___ here.   I don't be - long ___ here.

Additional Lyrics

3. I don't care if it hurts,
   I want to have control.
   I want a perfect body,
   I want a perfect soul.

4. I want you to notice
   When I'm not around.
   You're so fuckin' special,
   I wish I were special.

5. Whatever makes you happy,
   Whatever you want.
   You're so fuckin' special,
   I wish I were special.

Don't Fear the Reaper

Words and Music by Donald Roeser

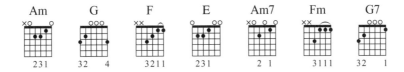

Strum Pattern: 3
Pick Pattern: 2

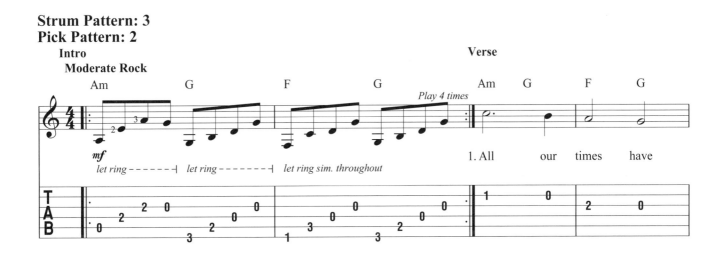

Copyright © 1976 Sony/ATV Music Publishing LLC
Copyright Renewed
All Rights Administered by Sony/ATV Music Publishing LLC, 424 Church Street, Suite 1200, Nashville, TN 37219
International Copyright Secured   All Rights Reserved

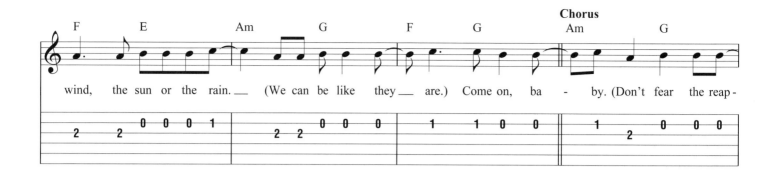

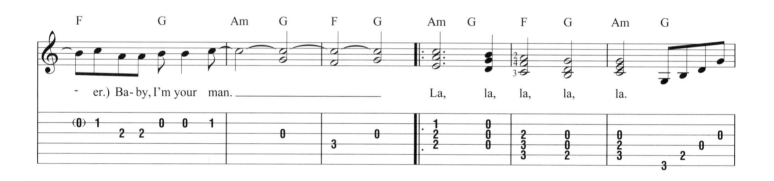

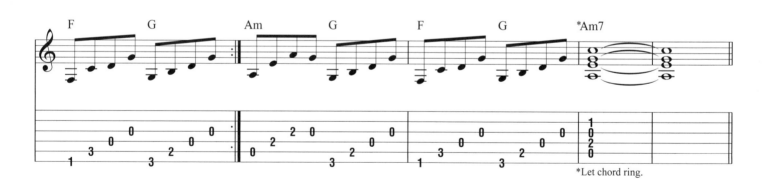

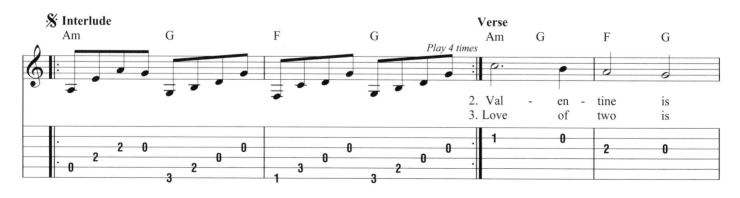

20

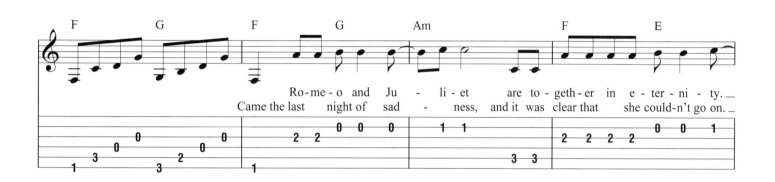

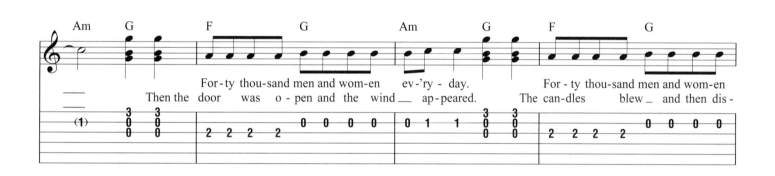

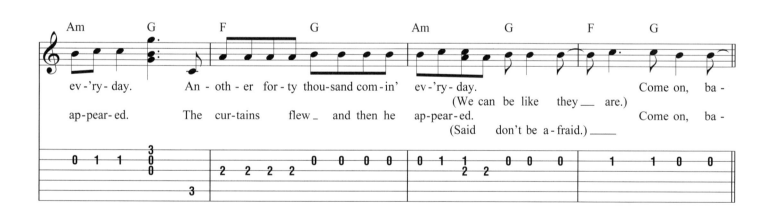

Chorus

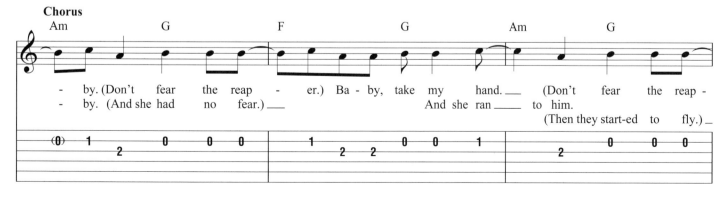

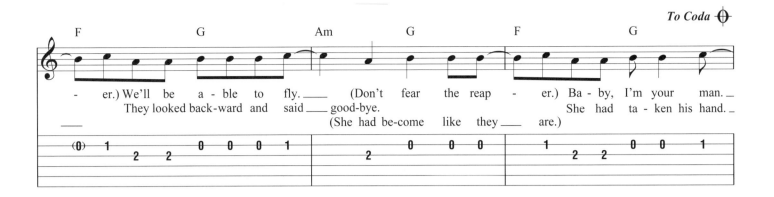

-er.) We'll be a - ble to fly.___ (Don't fear the reap - er.) Ba - by, I'm your man. _
They looked back-ward and said ___ good-bye.   She had ta - ken his hand. _
___   (She had be-come like they ___ are.)

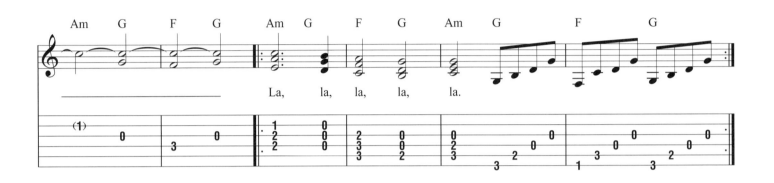

La, la, la, la, la.

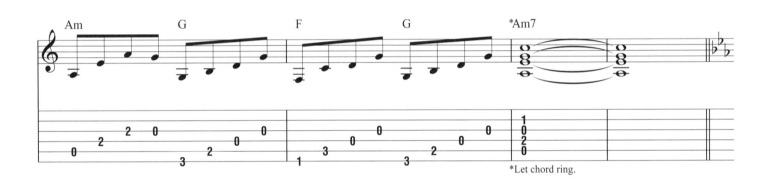

*Let chord ring.

Bridge
**N.C.(Fm)

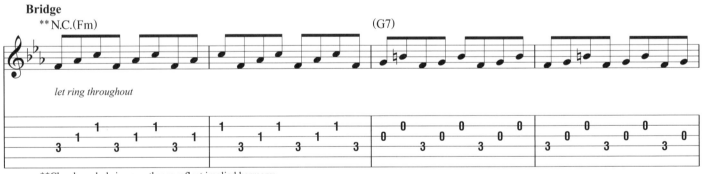

let ring throughout

**Chord symbols in parentheses reflect implied harmony.

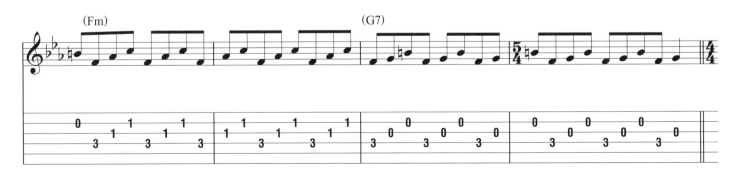

Guitar Solo

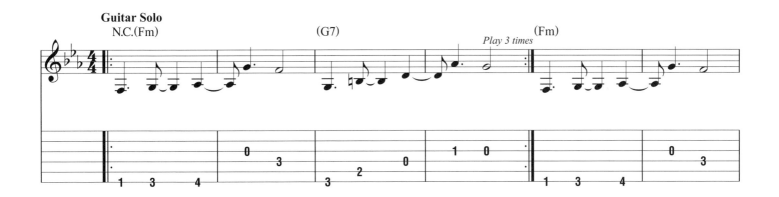

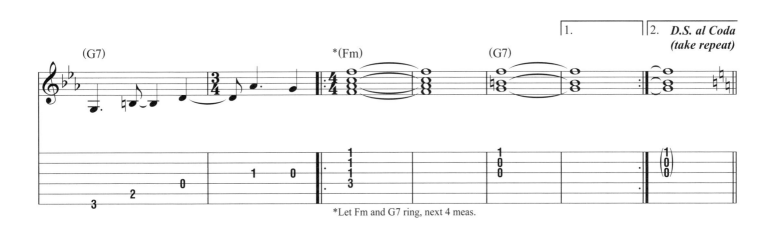

*Let Fm and G7 ring, next 4 meas.

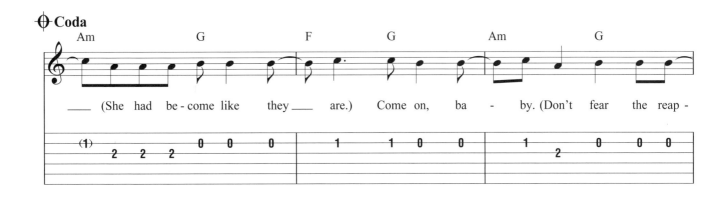

_____ (She had be - come like they _____ are.) Come on, ba - by. (Don't fear the reap -

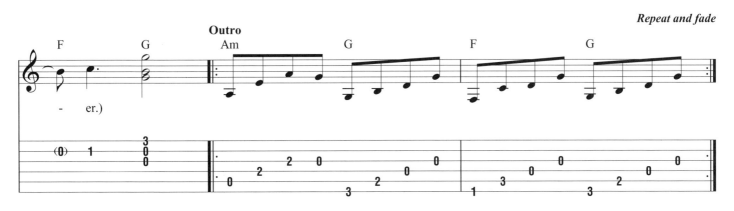

- er.)

Ding-Dong! The Witch Is Dead

from THE WIZARD OF OZ

Lyric by E.Y. "Yip" Harburg
Music by Harold Arlen

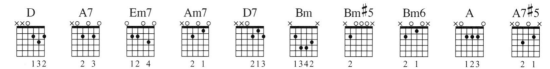

Strum Pattern: 5
Pick Pattern: 5

Verse
Moderately fast, in 2

1., 3. Ding - dong, the witch is dead! Which old witch? The

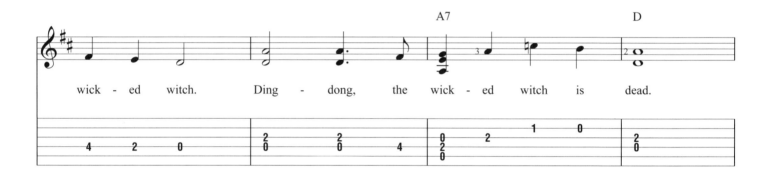

wick - ed witch. Ding - dong, the wick - ed witch is dead.

Wake up, you sleep - y head, rub your eyes, get

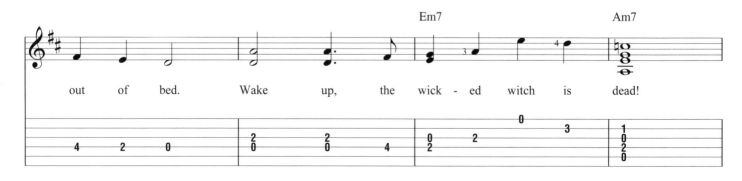

out of bed. Wake up, the wick - ed witch is dead!

© 1938 (Renewed) METRO-GOLDWYN-MAYER INC.
© 1939 (Renewed) EMI FEIST CATALOG INC.
All Rights Administered by EMI FEIST CATALOG INC. (Publishing) and ALFRED MUSIC (Print)
All Rights Reserved   Used by Permission

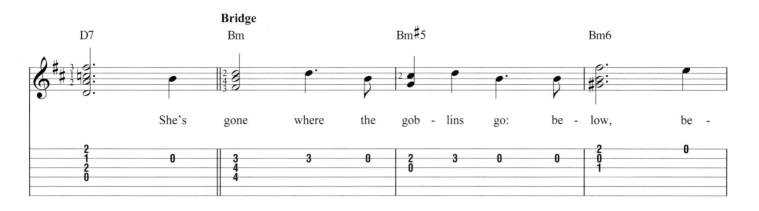

Bridge

D7   Bm   Bm#5   Bm6

She's gone where the gob - lins go: be - low, be -

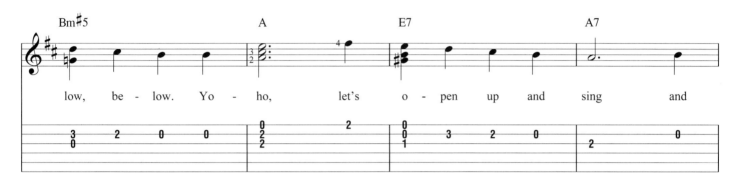

Bm#5   A   E7   A7

low, be - low. Yo - ho, let's o - pen up and sing and

Verse

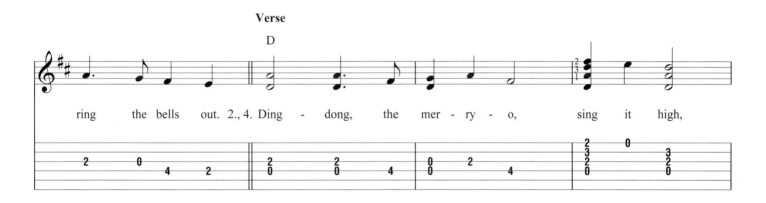

D

ring the bells out. 2., 4. Ding - dong, the mer - ry - o, sing it high,

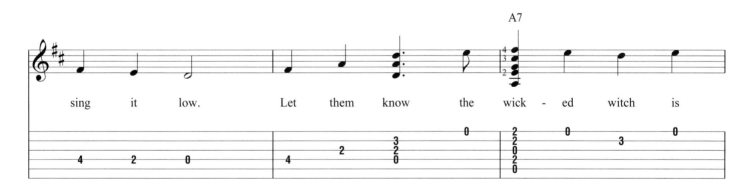

A7

sing it low. Let them know the wick - ed witch is

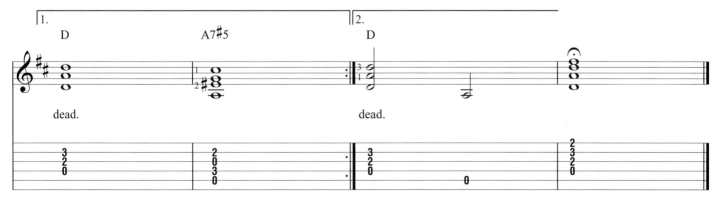

1.
D   A7#5   2.   D

dead.   dead.

Theme from "Dracula"

from DRACULA

Music by John Williams

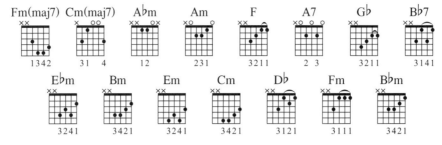

Strum Pattern: 3
Pick Pattern: 3

Intro
Moderately slow, in 2

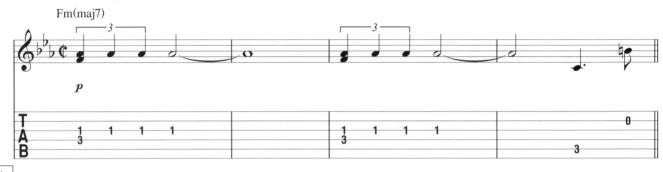

A

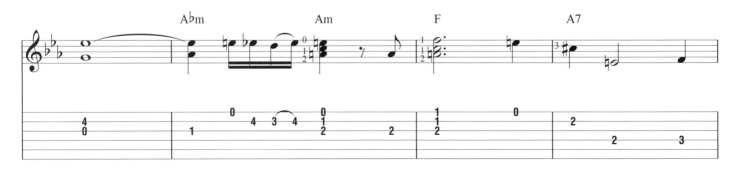

Copyright © 1979 USI B MUSIC PUBLISHING
All Rights Controlled and Administered by SONGS OF UNIVERSAL, INC.
All Rights Reserved   Used by Permission

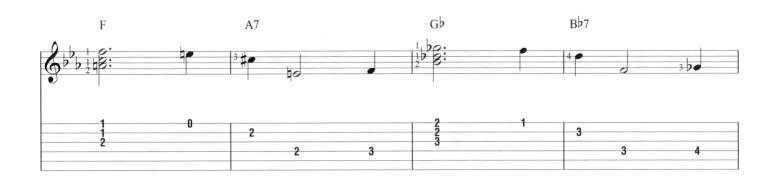

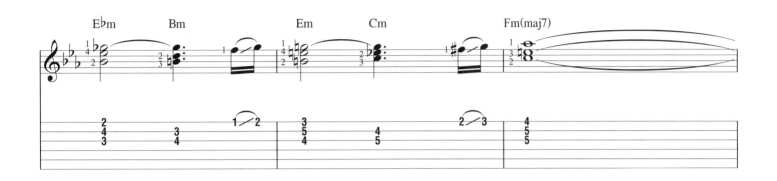

B

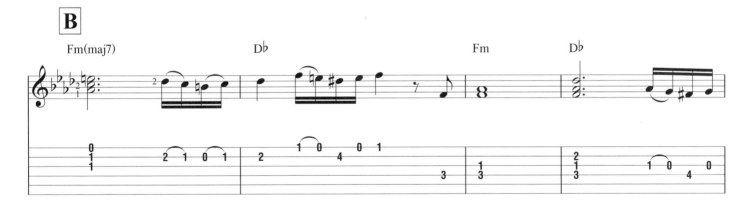

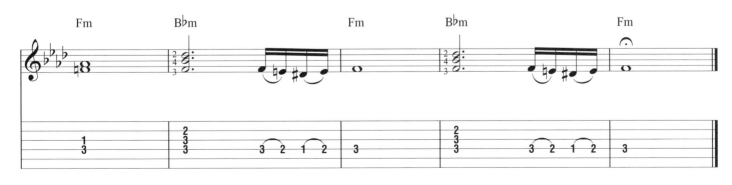

Every Day Is Halloween

Words and Music by Al Jourgensen

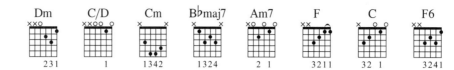

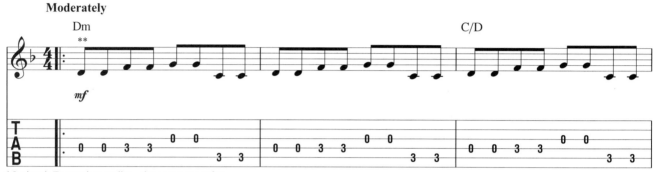

*Capo I

Strum Pattern: 1
Pick Pattern: 1

Intro
Moderately

*Optional: To match recording, place capo at 1st fret.

**Synth bass arr. for gtr., next 4 meas.

% Verse

N.C.(Dm)

1. Well, I live with snakes and liz-ards and
3. Well, I let their teen-y minds think that they're

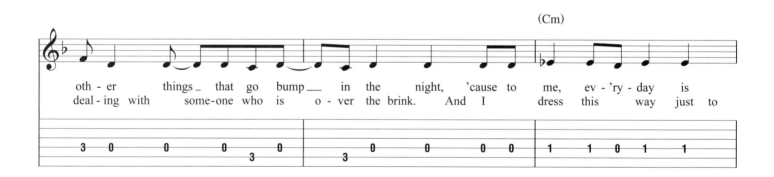

(Cm)

oth-er things___ that go bump___ in the night, 'cause to me, ev-'ry-day is
deal-ing with some-one who is o-ver the brink. And I dress this way just to

(Dm)

Hal-low-een.___ I've giv-en up hid-ing and start-ed to fight.___
keep them at bay, 'cause Hal-low-een is ev-'ry-day,___ hey.

Copyright © 1984 Lovolar Music
All Rights Administered by Bike Music c/o The Bicycle Music Company
All Rights Reserved   Used by Permission

Interlude

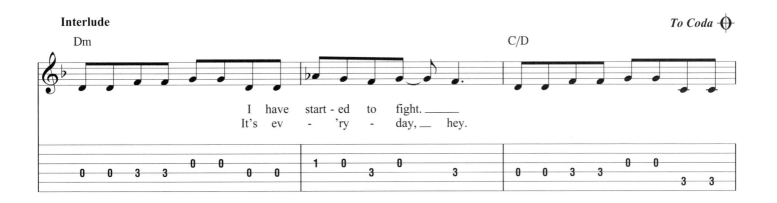

I have start - ed to fight. _____
It's ev - 'ry - day, __ hey.

Verse

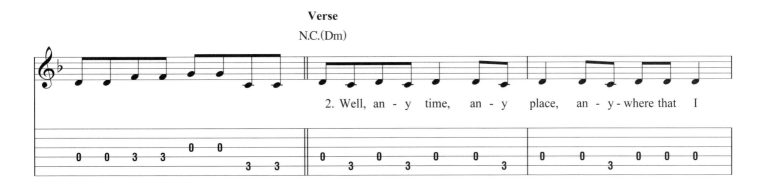

2. Well, an - y time, an - y place, an - y - where that I

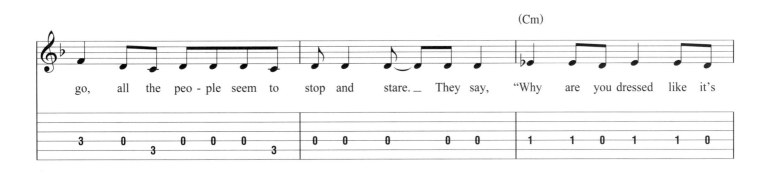

go, all the peo - ple seem to stop and stare. __ They say, "Why are you dressed like it's

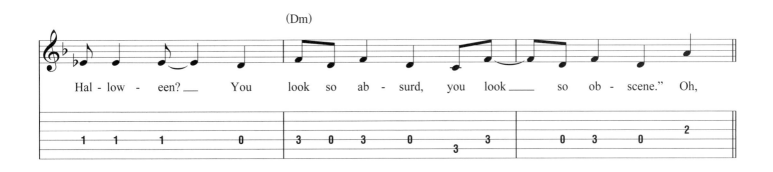

Hal - low - een? __ You look so ab - surd, you look __ so ob - scene." Oh,

Chorus

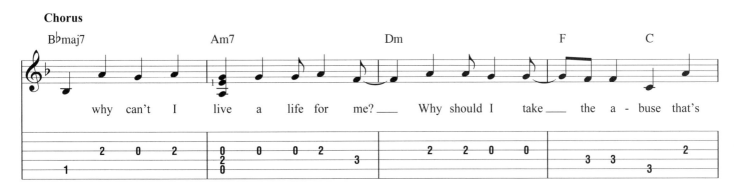

why can't I live a life for me? __ Why should I take __ the a - buse that's

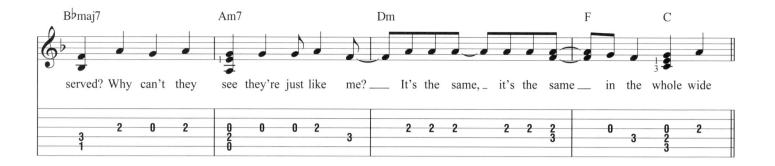

served? Why can't they see they're just like me?___ It's the same, _ it's the same _ in the whole wide

Interlude

D.S. al Coda

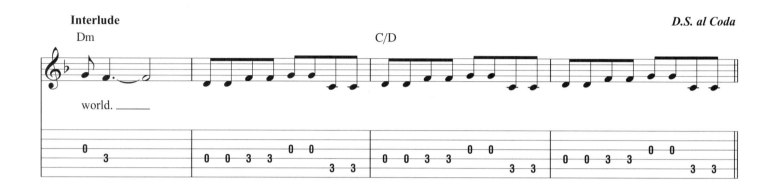

world. _____

⊕ **Coda**

Chorus

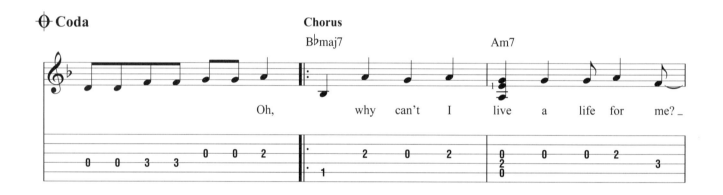

Oh, why can't I live a life for me?_

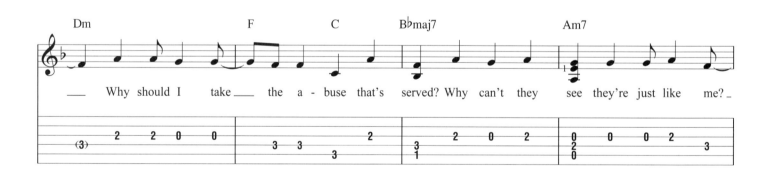

___ Why should I take ___ the a - buse that's served? Why can't they see they're just like me?_

1.

Interlude

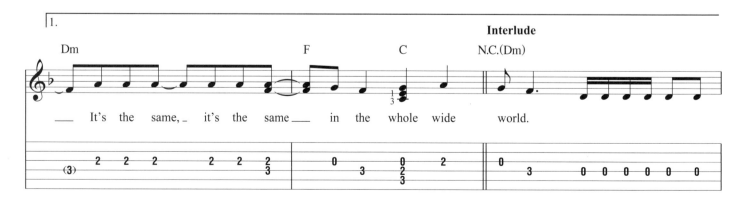

___ It's the same, _ it's the same ___ in the whole wide world.

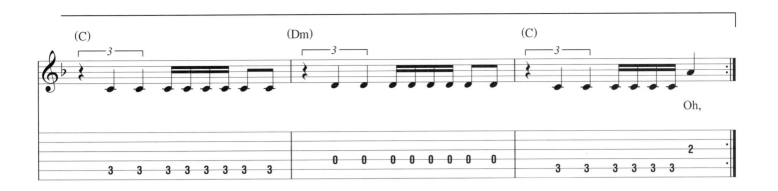

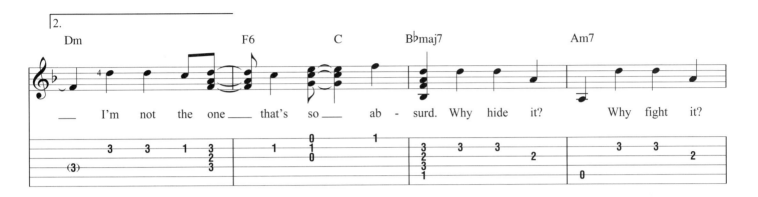

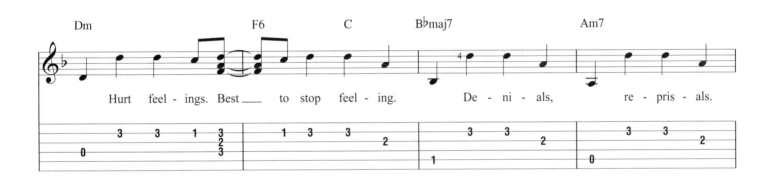

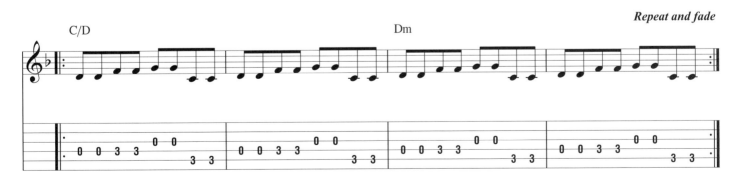

Fear of the Dark

Words and Music by Steven Harris

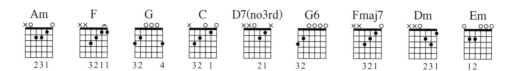

*Capo V

Strum Pattern: 5
Pick Pattern: 1

Verse
Moderately fast

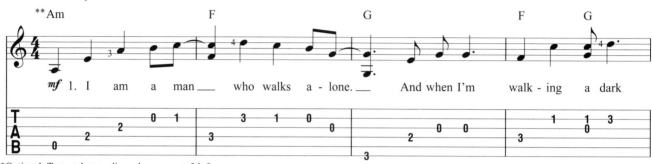

*Optional: To match recording, place capo at 5th fret.
**Chord symbols reflect implied harmony.

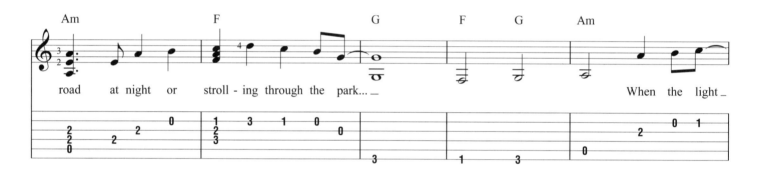

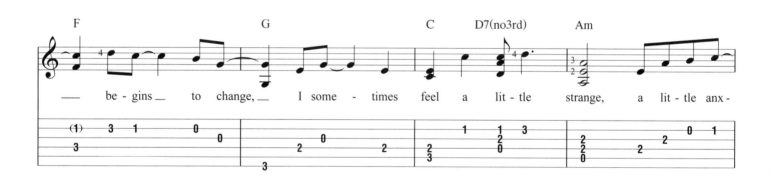

Copyright © 1992 by Iron Maiden Holdings Ltd.
All Rights in the United States and Canada Administered by Universal Music - Z Tunes LLC
International Copyright Secured   All Rights Reserved

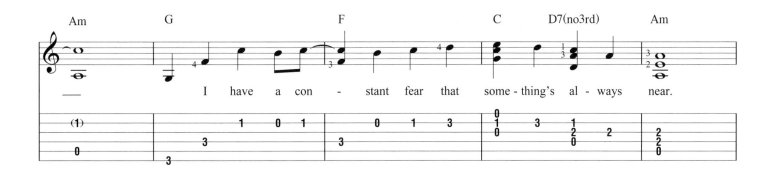

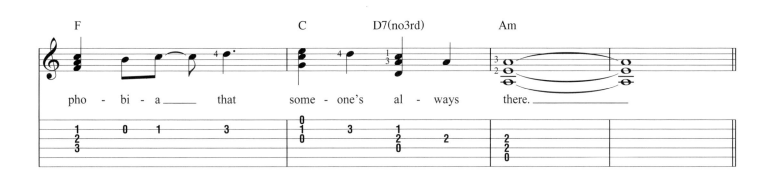

Verse
Faster

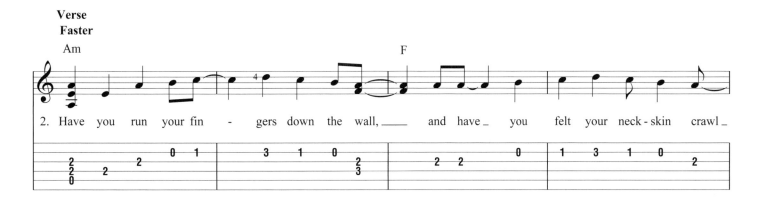

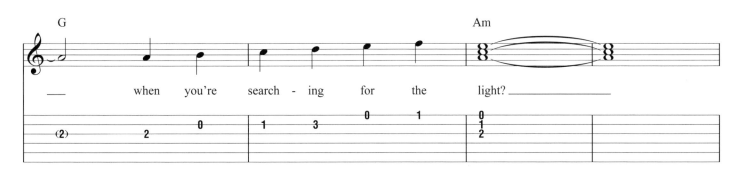

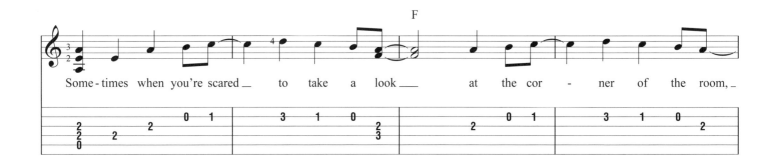

Some-times when you're scared __ to take a look __ at the cor - ner of the room, __

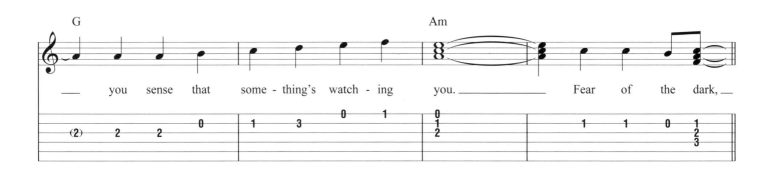

__ you sense that some - thing's watch - ing you. _____ Fear of the dark, __

𝄉 Chorus

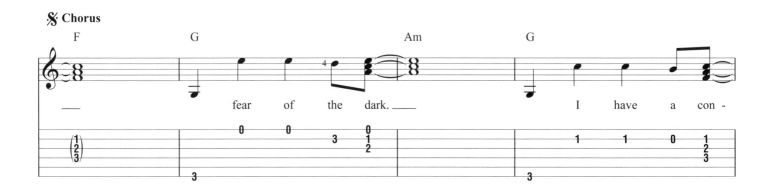

__ fear of the dark. ___ I have a con -

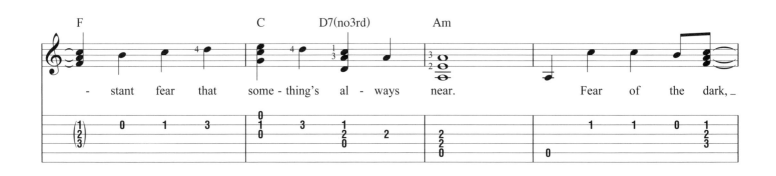

- stant fear that some - thing's al - ways near. Fear of the dark, __

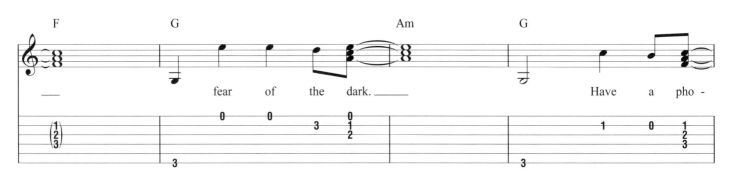

__ fear of the dark. ___ Have a pho -

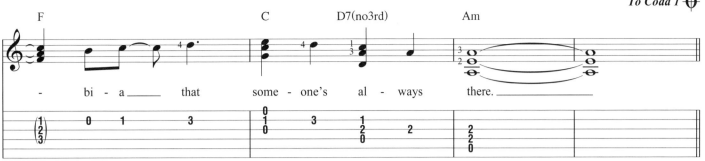

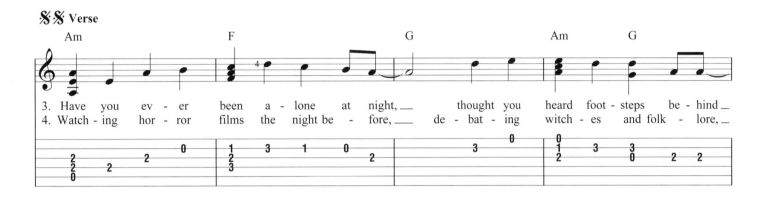

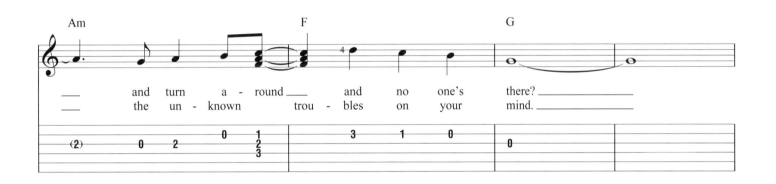

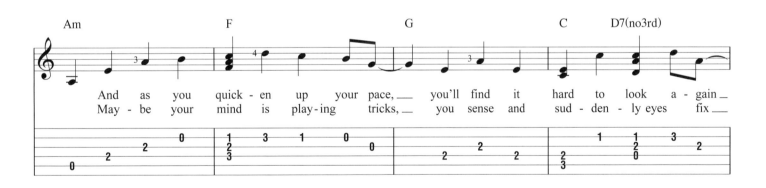

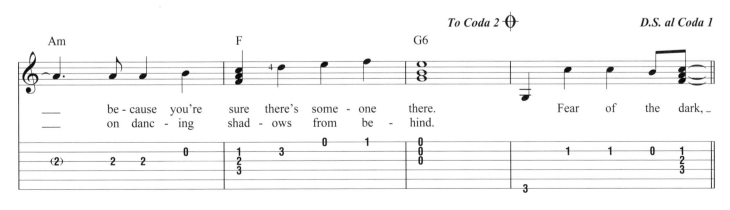

⊕ Coda 1

Bridge

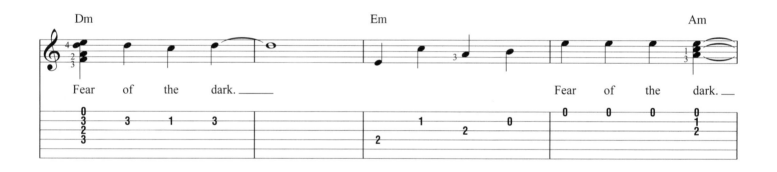

2nd time, D.S.S. al Coda 2

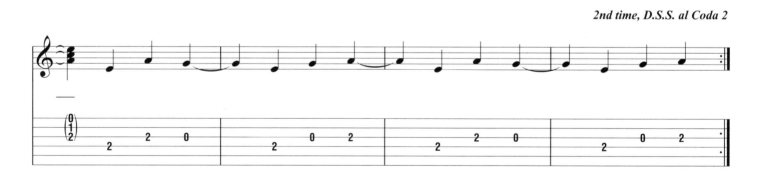

⊕ Coda 2

Chorus

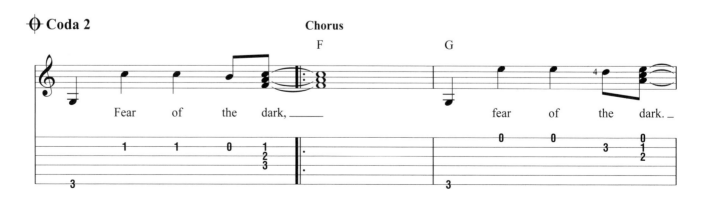

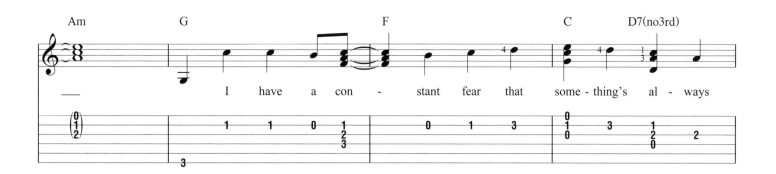

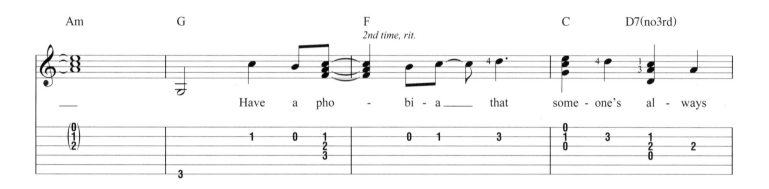

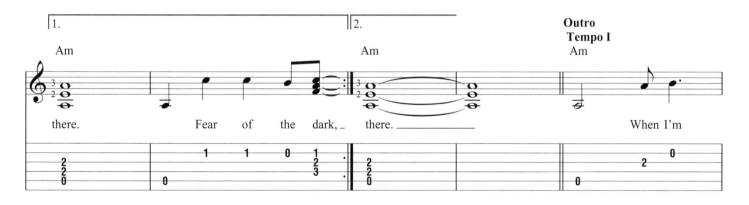

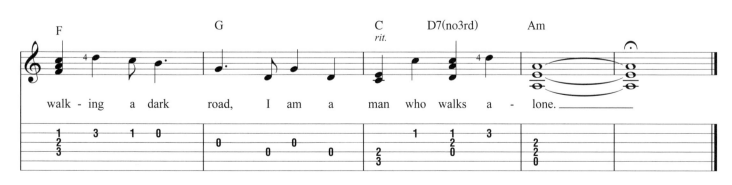

Fog Bound

from Walt Disney Pictures' PIRATES OF THE CARIBBEAN: THE CURSE OF THE BLACK PEARL
Music by Klaus Badelt

© 2003 Walt Disney Music Company
All Rights Reserved   Used by Permission

Frankenstein

By Edgar Winter

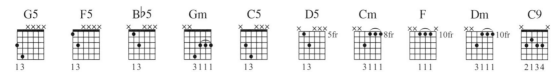

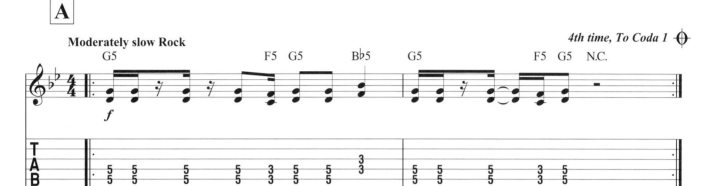

Strum Pattern: 1

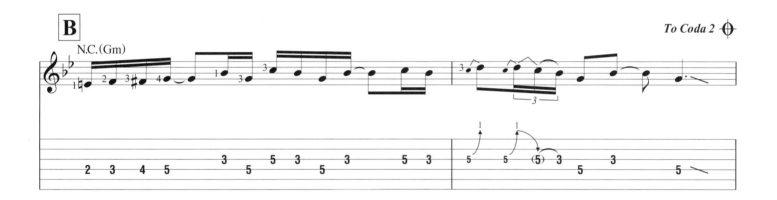

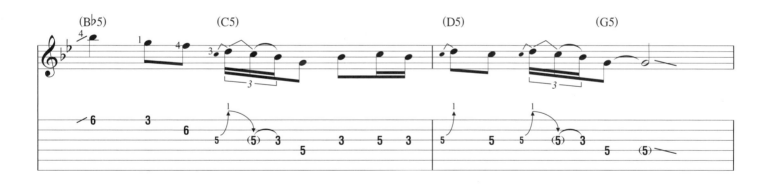

Copyright © 1972 EMI Longitude Music
Copyright Renewed
All Rights Administered by Sony/ATV Music Publishing LLC, 424 Church Street, Suite 1200, Nashville, TN 37219
International Copyright Secured   All Rights Reserved

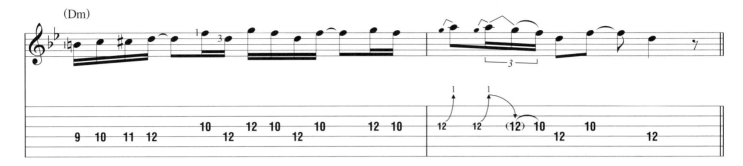

2nd time, D.C. al Coda 1
(take repeat)

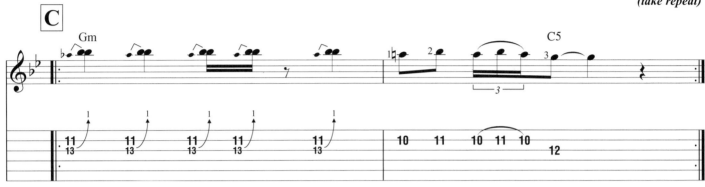

$\oplus$ **Coda 1**

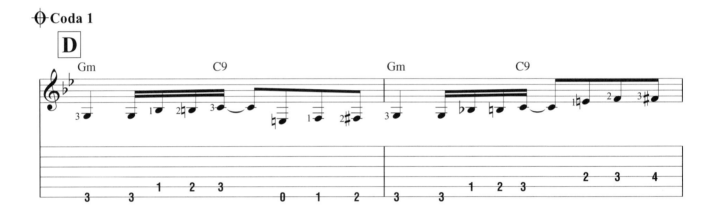

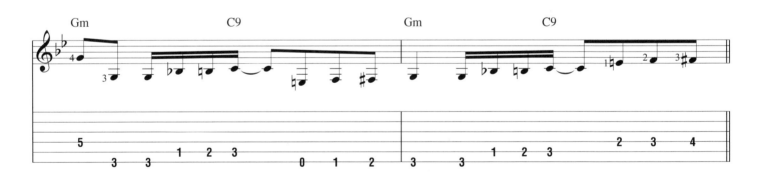

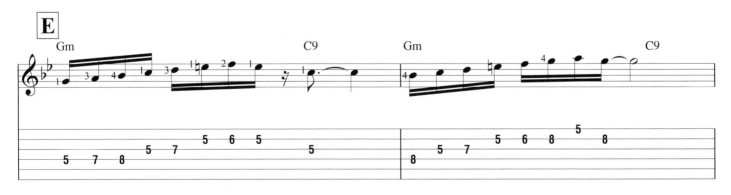

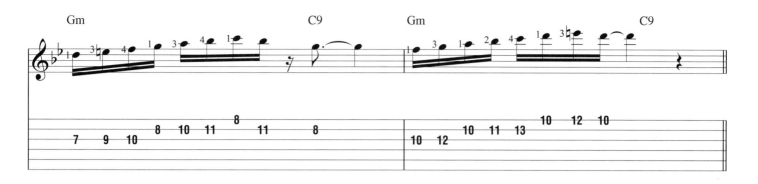

2nd time, D.C. al Coda 2
(take repeat)

F

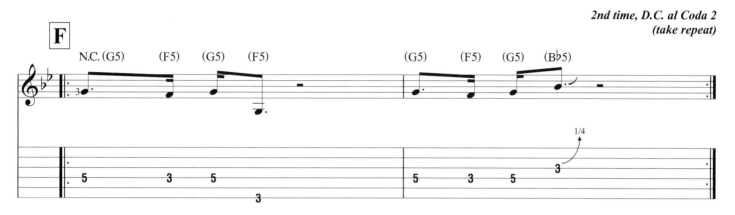

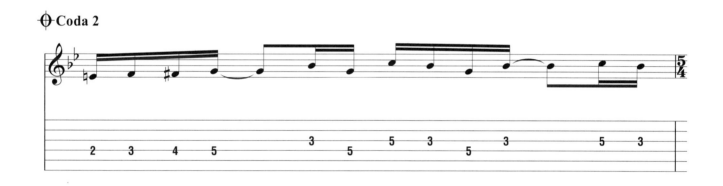

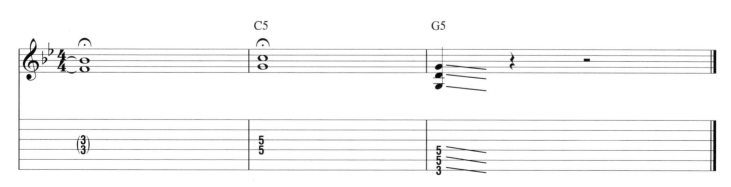

Friday the 13th Theme

Written by Harry Manfredini

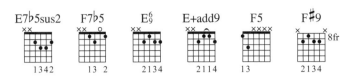

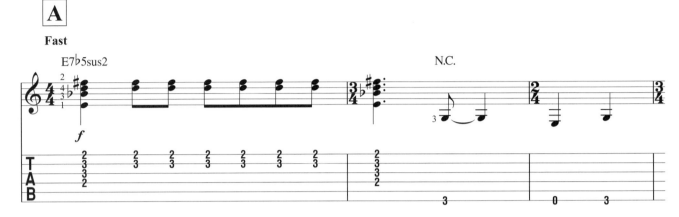

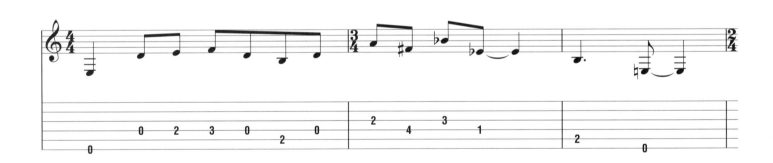

Copyright © 1980 Sony/ATV Music Publishing LLC
All Rights Administered by Sony/ATV Music Publishing LLC, 424 Church Street, Suite 1200, Nashville, TN 37219
International Copyright Secured   All Rights Reserved

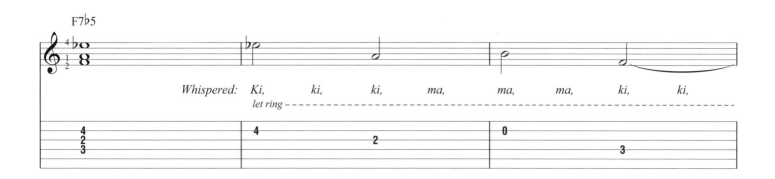

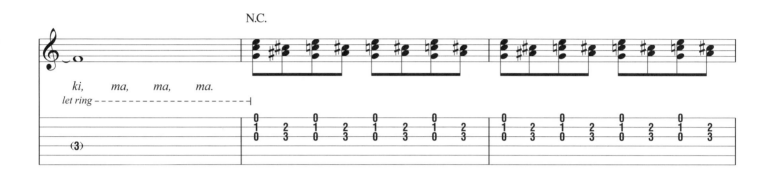

B

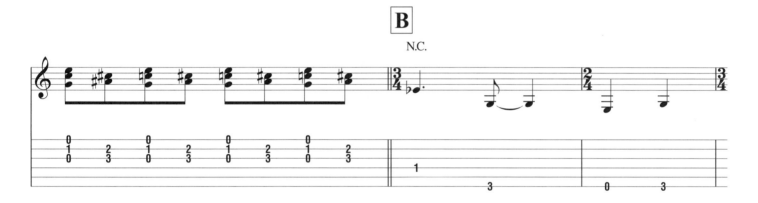

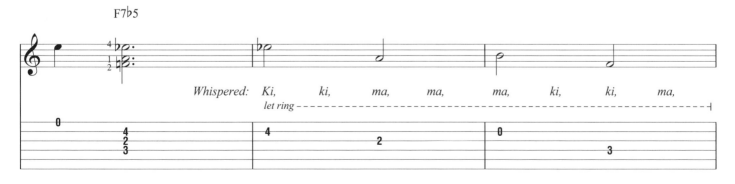

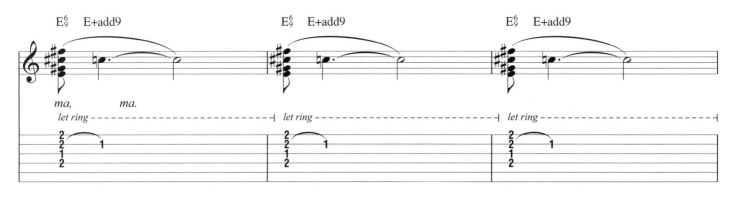

C

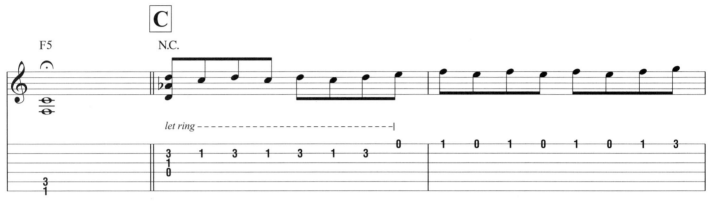

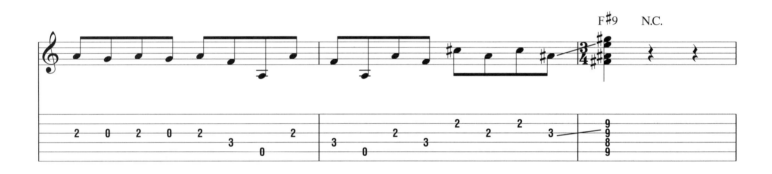

*P.S.   Whispered: Ki, ki, ki, ma,   ma,   ma,   ki,

*Scrape 6th string w/ pick toward bridge.

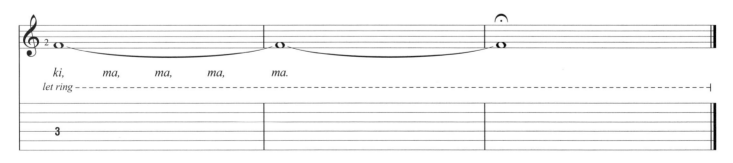

Halloween Song

Traditional

Strum Pattern: 8
Pick Pattern: 8

Verse
Moderately slow, in 2

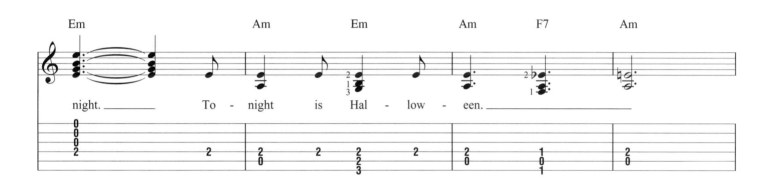

Gob - lins and witch - es ride on a broom. Ghost - ly shad - ows steal 'round the room to -

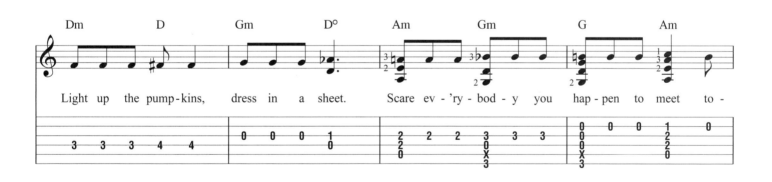

night. _____ To - night is Hal - low - een. _____

Light up the pump - kins, dress in a sheet. Scare ev - 'ry - bod - y you hap - pen to meet to -

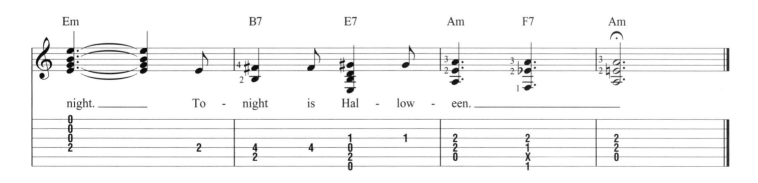

night. _____ To - night is Hal - low - een. _____

Copyright © 2015 by HAL LEONARD CORPORATION
International Copyright Secured   All Rights Reserved

Funeral March

from PIANO SONATA IN B-FLAT MINOR, OP. 35
By Fryderyk Chopin

Strum Pattern: 3
Pick Pattern: 3

Copyright © 2015 by HAL LEONARD CORPORATION
International Copyright Secured   All Rights Reserved

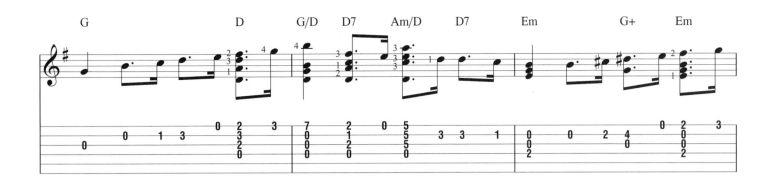

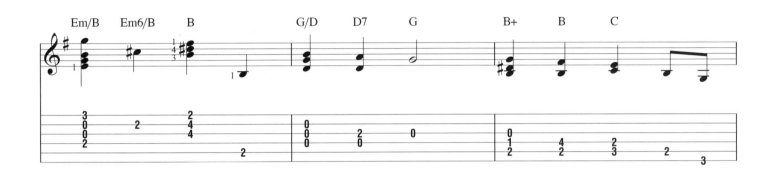

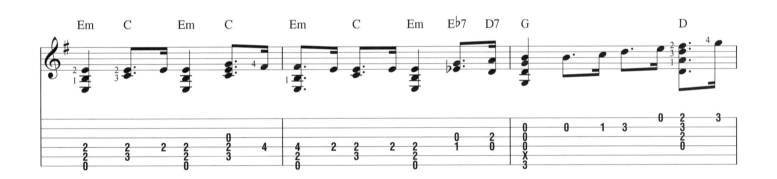

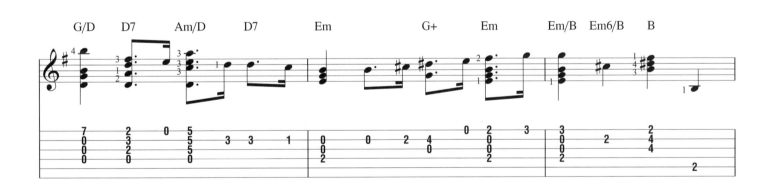

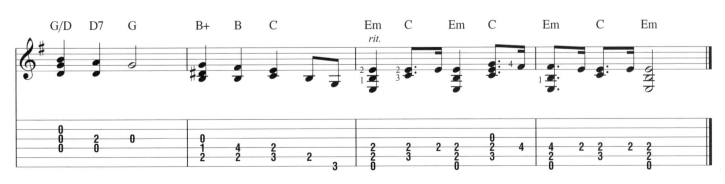

Funeral March of a Marionette

By Charles Gounod

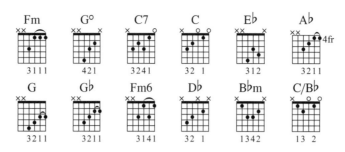

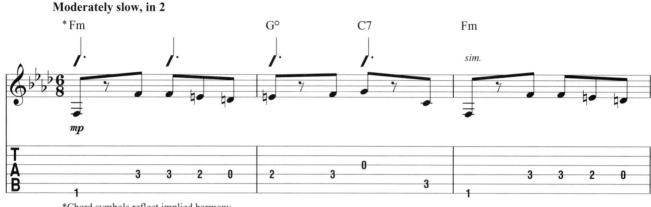

Moderately slow, in 2

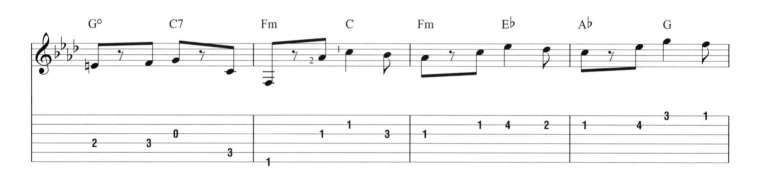

*Chord symbols reflect implied harmony.

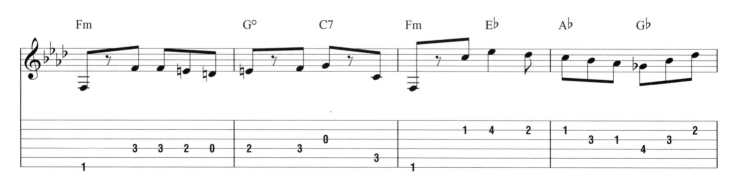

Copyright © 2015 by HAL LEONARD CORPORATION
International Copyright Secured   All Rights Reserved

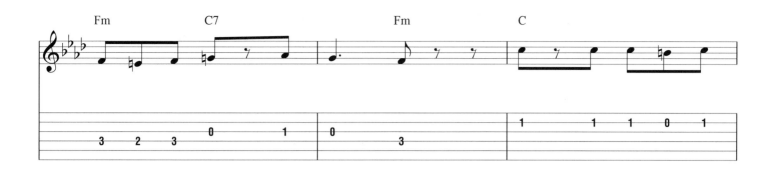

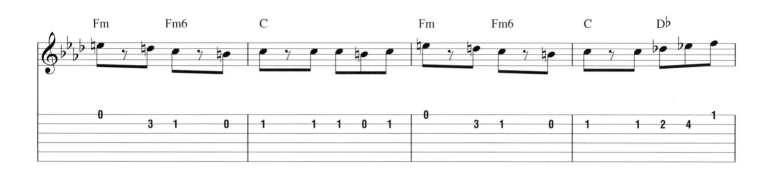

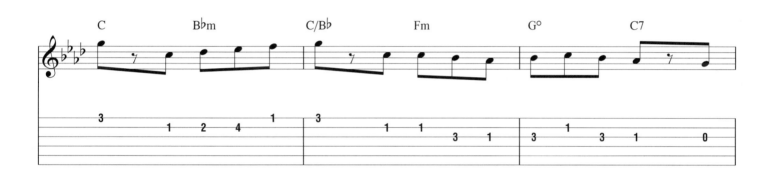

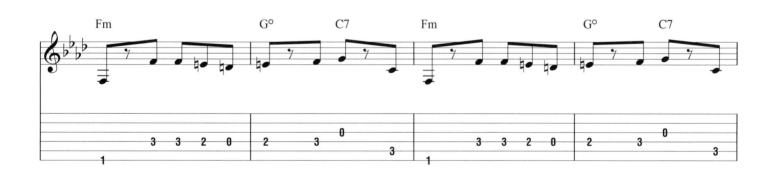

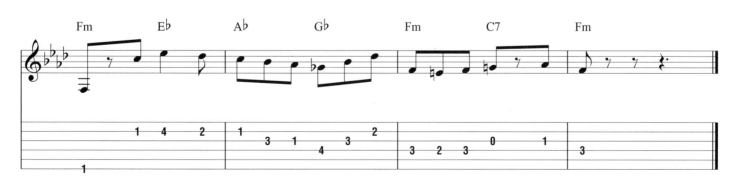

Ghostbusters

from the Columbia Motion Picture GHOSTBUSTERS
Words and Music by Ray Parker, Jr.

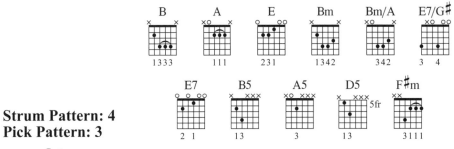

Strum Pattern: 4
Pick Pattern: 3

Intro
Moderately

N.C.

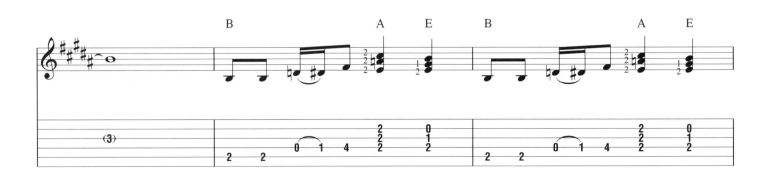

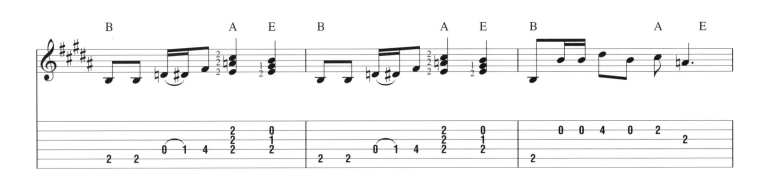

Spoken: (Ghost - bust- ers!)

1. If there's

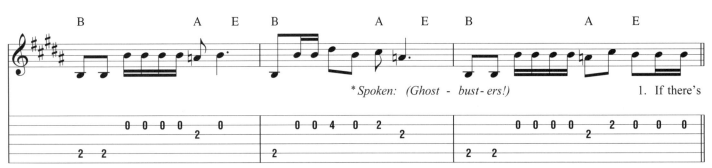

*Lyrics in italics are spoken throughout.

© 1984 EMI GOLDEN TORCH MUSIC CORP. and RAYDIOLA MUSIC
Exclusive Print Rights for EMI GOLDEN TORCH MUSIC CORP. Administered by ALFRED MUSIC
All Rights Reserved   Used by Permission

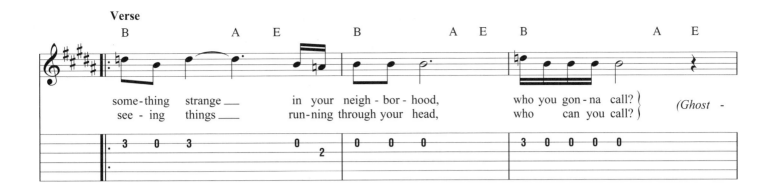

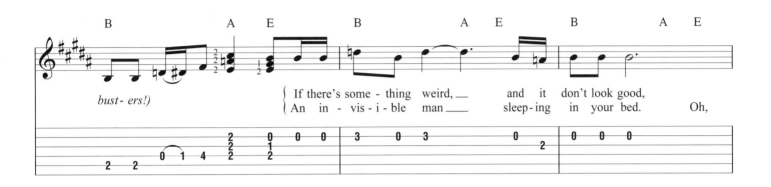

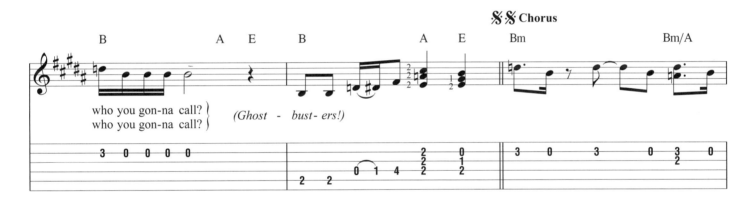

Additional Lyrics

4. If you have a dose
   Of a freaky ghost, baby,
   You'd better call... *(Ghostbusters!)*

5. When it comes through your door,
   Unless you just want some more,
   I think you'd better call... *(Ghostbusters!)*

Highway to Hell

Words and Music by Angus Young, Malcolm Young and Bon Scott

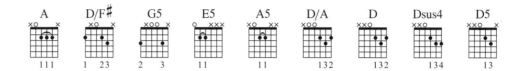

Strum Pattern: 5
Pick Pattern: 1

Intro
Moderate Rock

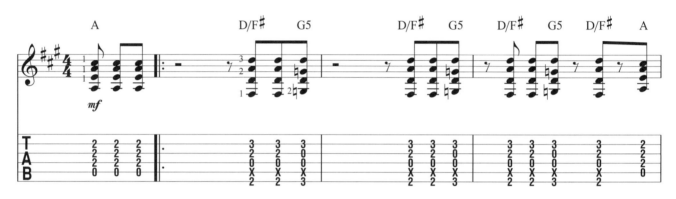

Verse
w/ Intro pattern

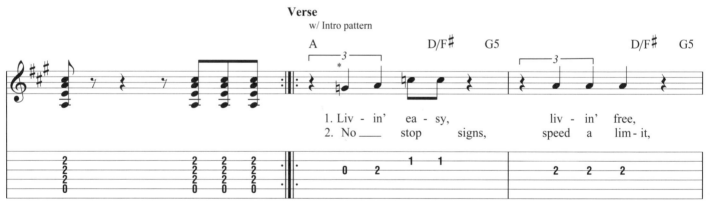

*Sung one octave higher throughout, except where noted.

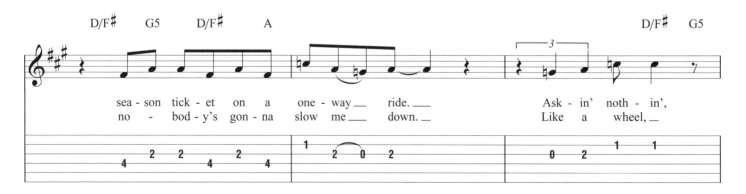

Copyright © 1979 by J. Albert & Son Pty., Ltd.
International Copyright Secured   All Rights Reserved

*Lyrics in italics are spoken throughout.

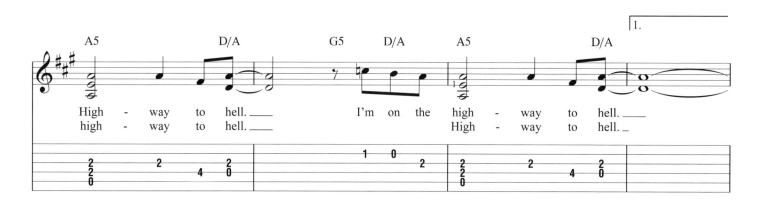

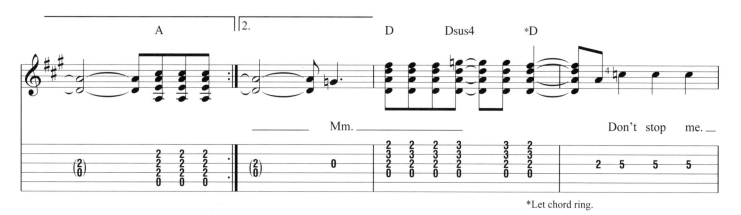

*Let chord ring.

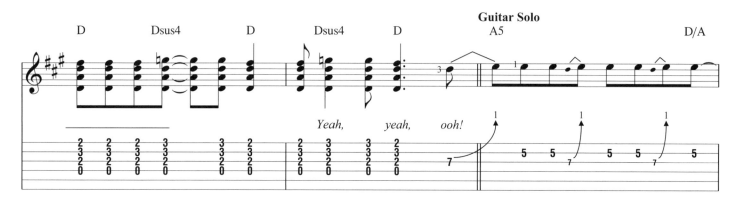

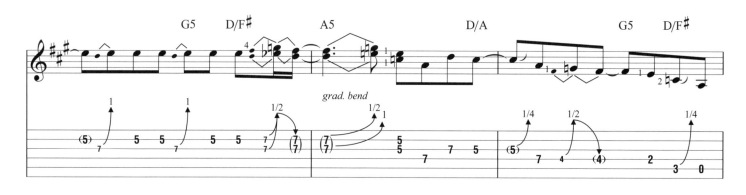

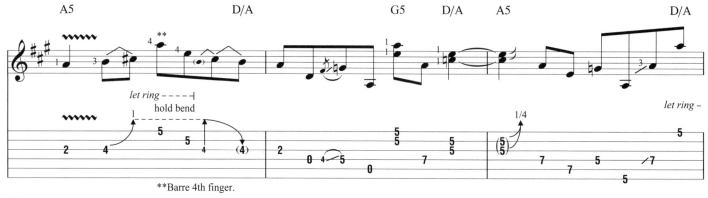

**Barre 4th finger.

56

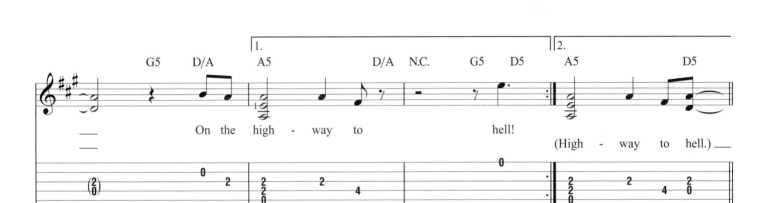

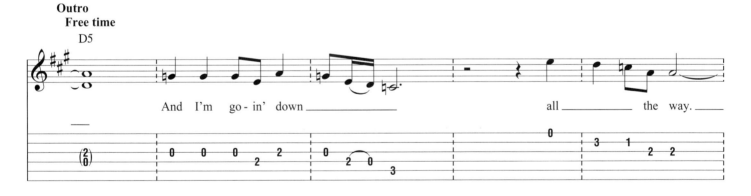

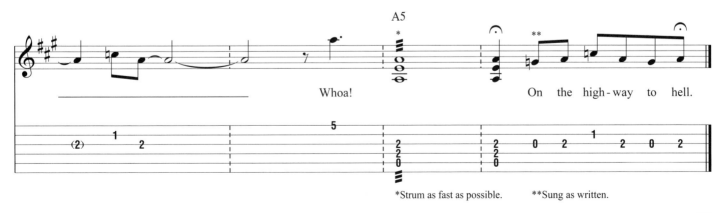

*Strum as fast as possible.   **Sung as written.

I Put a Spell on You

Words and Music by Jay Hawkins

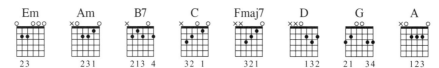

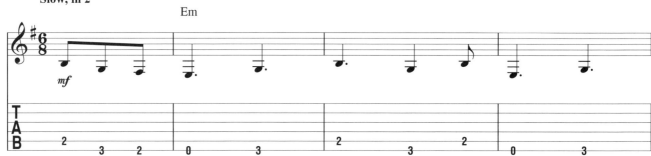

Strum Pattern: 8
Pick Pattern: 8

Intro
Slow, in 2

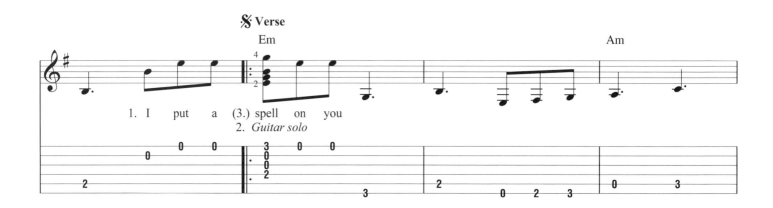

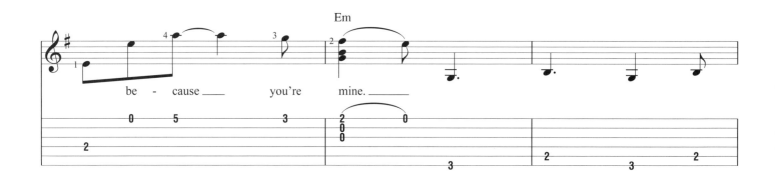

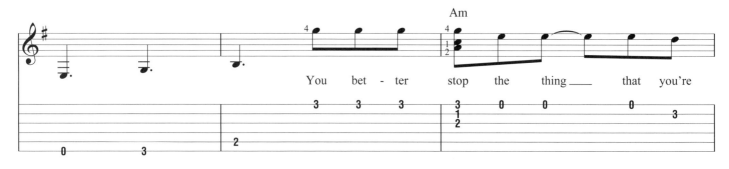

© 1956 (Renewed) EMI UNART CATALOG INC.
Exclusive Print Rights Controlled and Administered by ALFRED MUSIC
All Rights Reserved   Used by Permission

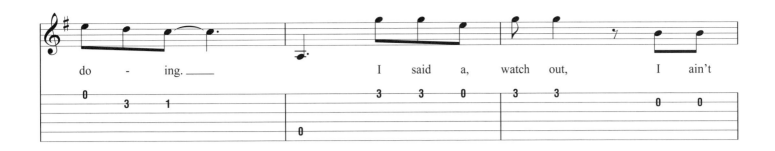

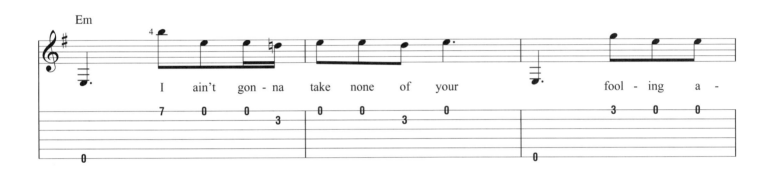

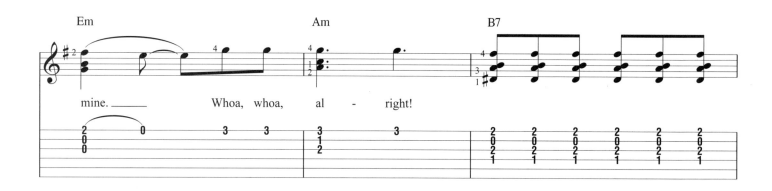

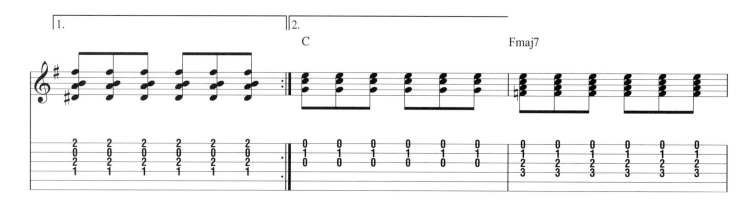

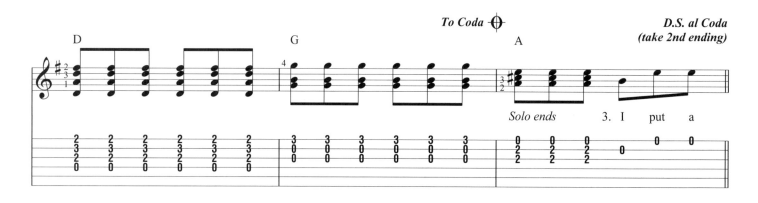

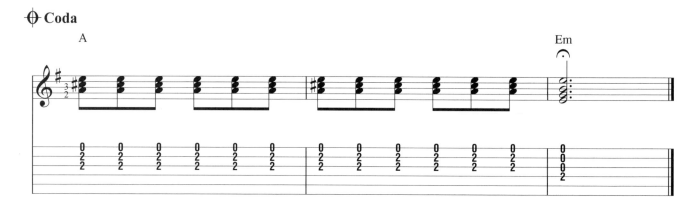

Theme from "Jaws"

from the Universal Picture JAWS

By John Williams

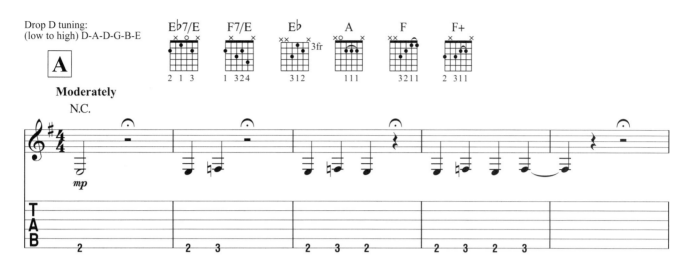

Drop D tuning:
(low to high) D-A-D-G-B-E

Moderately
N.C.

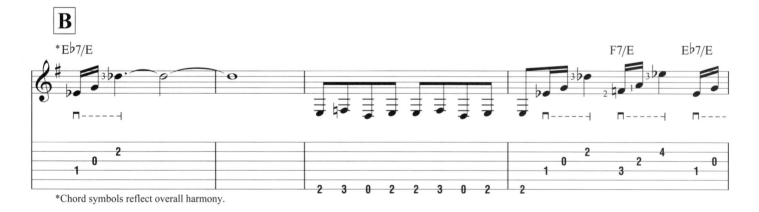

*Chord symbols reflect overall harmony.

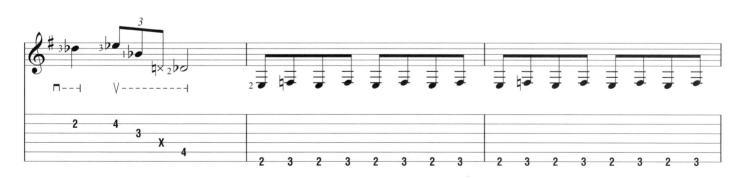

Copyright © 1975 USI B MUSIC PUBLISHING
Copyright Renewed
All Rights Controlled and Administered by SONGS OF UNIVERSAL, INC.
All Rights Reserved   Used by Permission

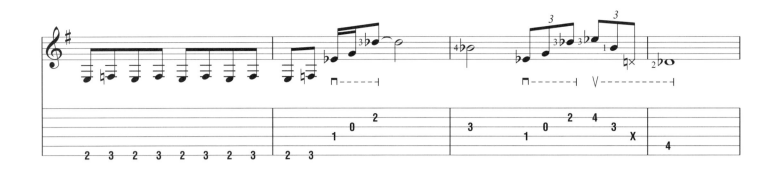

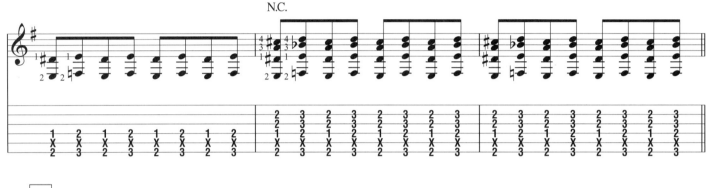

C

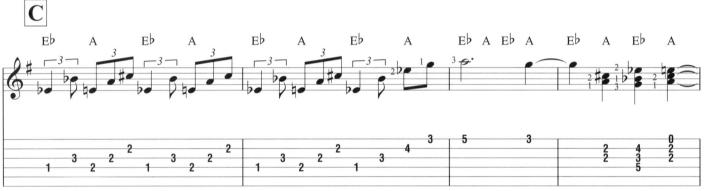

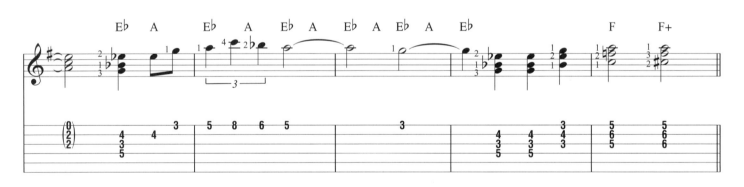

D

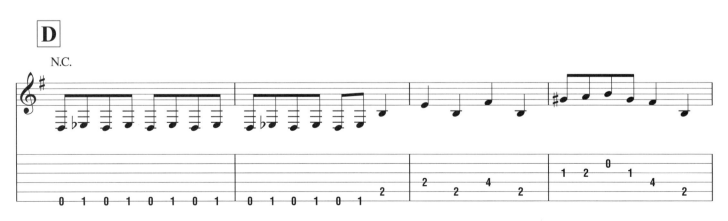

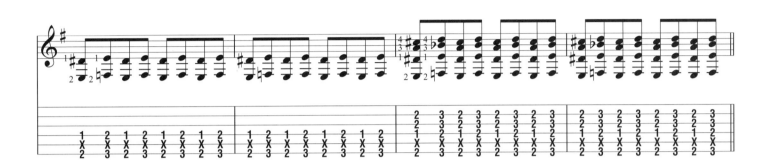

E

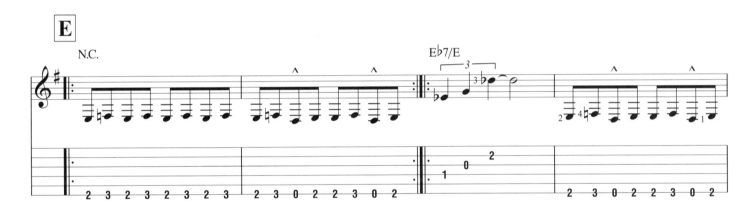

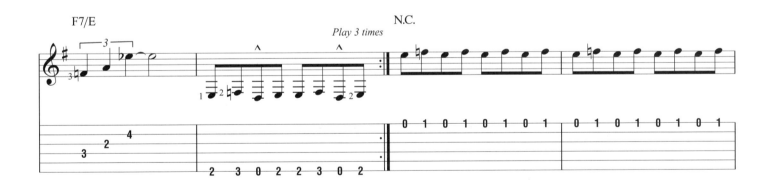

Monster Mash

Words and Music by Bobby Pickett and Leonard Capizzi

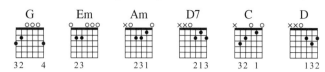

Strum Pattern: 5
Pick Pattern: 1

Verse

Moderately fast

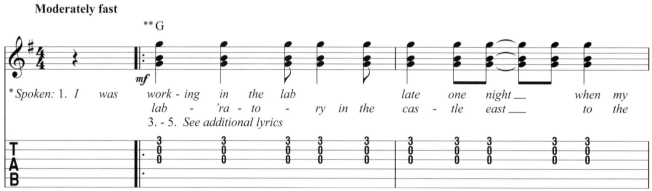

Spoken: 1. *I was work-ing in the lab late one night when my*
lab - 'ra - to - ry in the cas - tle east to the
3. - 5. *See additional lyrics*

*Lyrics in italics are spoken throughout.

**Chord symbols reflect basic harmony.

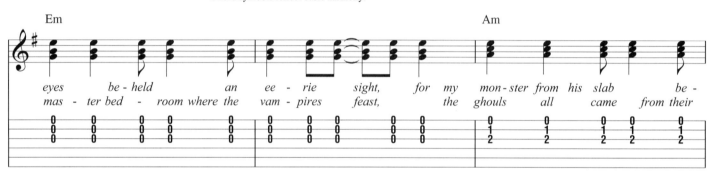

eyes be - held an ee - rie sight, for my mon - ster from his slab be -
mas - ter bed - room where the vam - pires feast, the ghouls all came from their

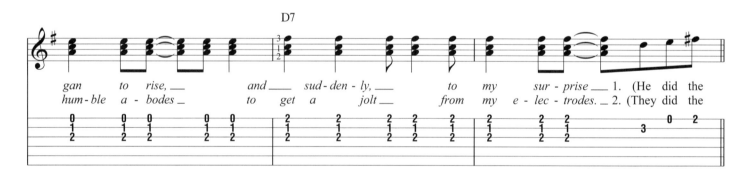

gan to rise, and sud - den - ly, to my sur - prise 1. (He did the
hum - ble a - bodes to get a jolt from my e - lec - trodes. 2. (They did the

Chorus

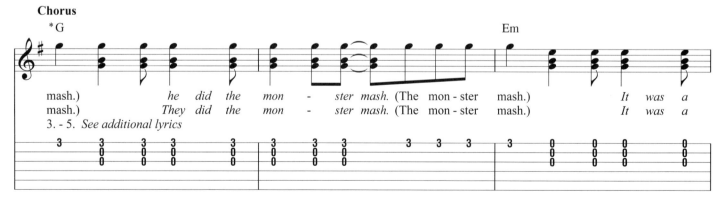

mash.) *he did the mon - ster mash. (The mon - ster mash.) It was a*
mash.) *They did the mon - ster mash. (The mon - ster mash.) It was a*
3. - 5. *See additional lyrics*

© 1962, 1963 (Renewed) RESERVOIR 416, HOUSE OF PAXTON MUSIC PRESS and CAPIZZI MUSIC CO.
All Rights for RESERVOIR 416 and HOUSE OF PAXTON MUSIC PRESS Administered by
RESERVOIR MEDIA MANAGEMENT, INC. (Publishing) and ALFRED MUSIC (Print)
All Rights for the world outside the U.S. and Canada Administered by UNICHAPPELL MUSIC, INC.
All Rights Reserved   Used by Permission

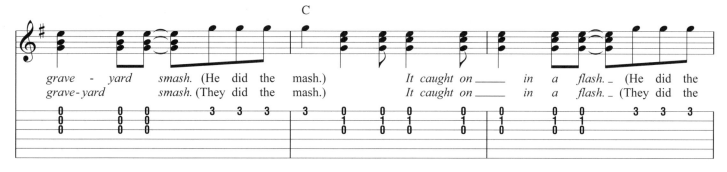

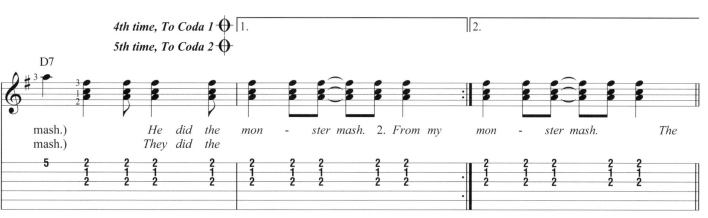

Bridge

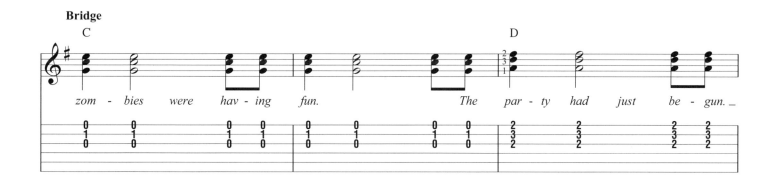

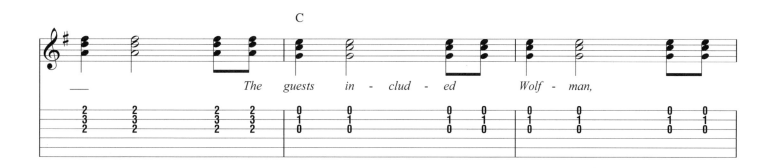

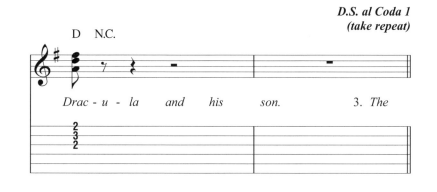

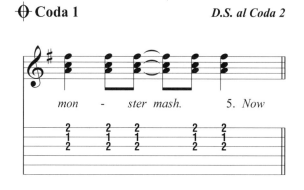

⊕ Coda 2

Outro
w/ Lead Voc. ad lib.

mon - ster mash.

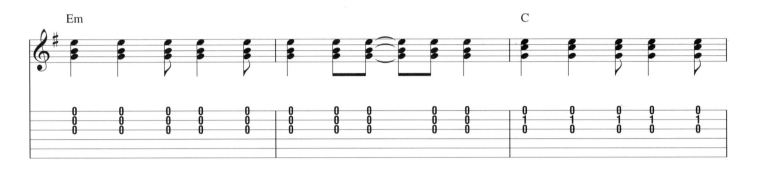

Repeat and fade

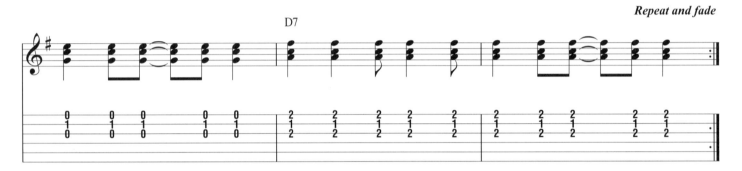

Additional Lyrics

3. *The scene was rockin'. All were digging the sounds.*
   Igor on chains, backed by his baying hounds.
   The coffin-bangers were about to arrive
   With their vocal group, "The Crypt-Kicker Five."

Chorus 3 (They played the mash.) *They played the monster mash.*
   (The monster mash.) *It was a graveyard smash.*
   (They played the mash.) *It caught on in a flash.*
   (They played the mash.) *They played the monster mash.*

4. *Out from his coffin, Drac's voice did ring.*
   Seems he was troubled by just one thing.
   He opened the lid and shook his fist
   And said, "Whatever happened to my Transylvanian Twist?"

Chorus 4 (It's now the mash.) *It's now the monster mash,*
   (The monster mash.) *And it's a graveyard smash.*
   (It's now the mash.) *It's caught on in a flash.*
   (It's now the mash.) *It's now the monster mash.*

5. *Now everything's cool, Drac's a part of the band,*
   And my monster mash is the hit of the land.
   For you, the living, this mash was meant, too.
   When you get to my door, tell them Boris sent you.

Chorus 5 (Then you can mash.) *Then you can monster mash*
   (The monster mash.) *And do my graveyard smash.*
   (Then you can mash.) *You'll catch on in a flash.*
   (Then you can mash.) *Then you can monster mash.*

Nightmare on Elm Street

By Charles Bernstein

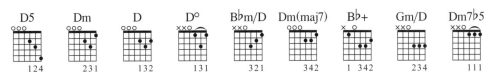

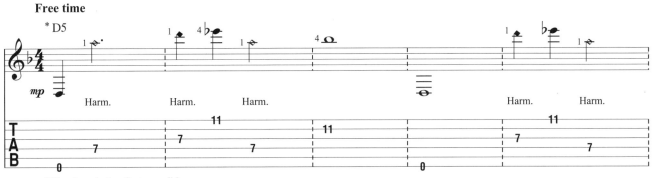

Drop D tuning:
(low to high) D-A-D-G-B-E

Free time

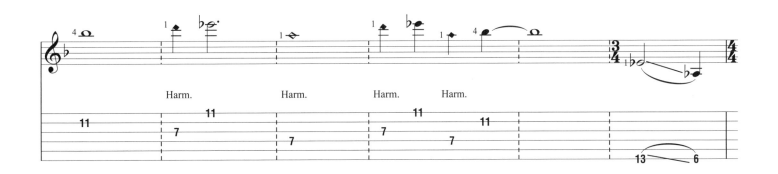

*Chord symbols reflect overall harmony.

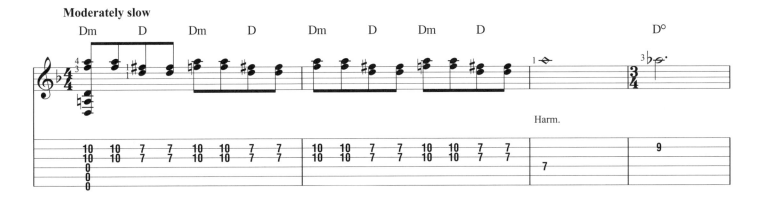

Moderately slow

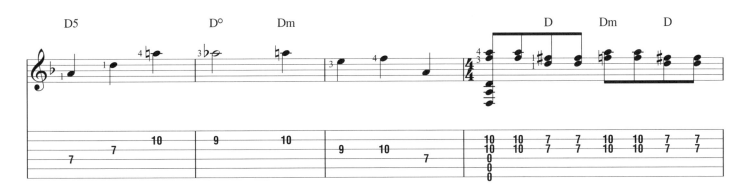

Copyright © 1984 NEW LINE TUNES
All Rights Controlled and Administered by UNIVERSAL MUSIC CORP.
All Rights Reserved   Used by Permission

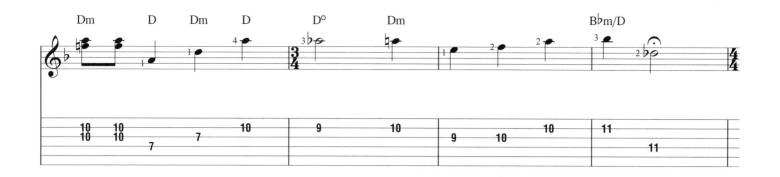

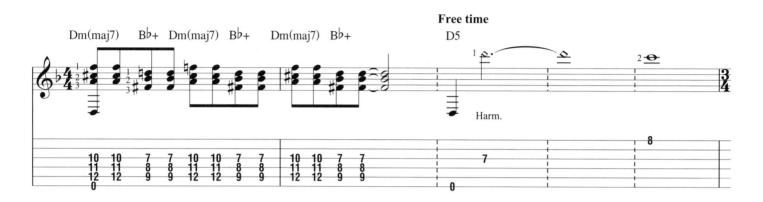

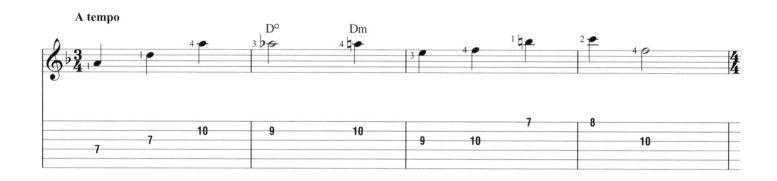

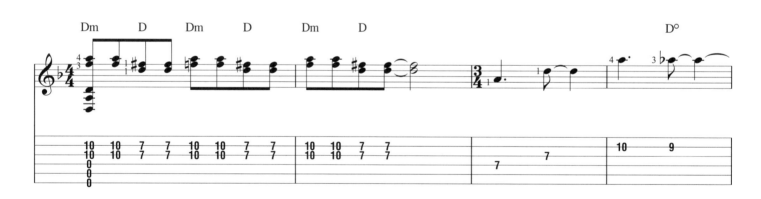

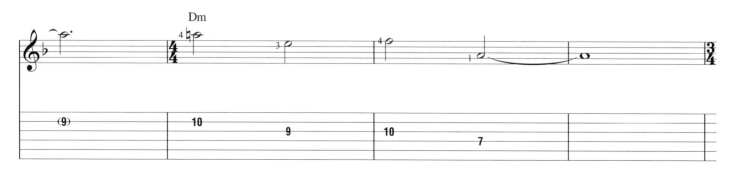

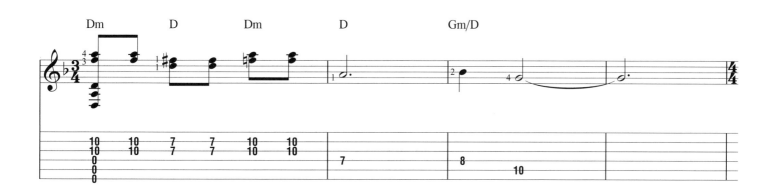

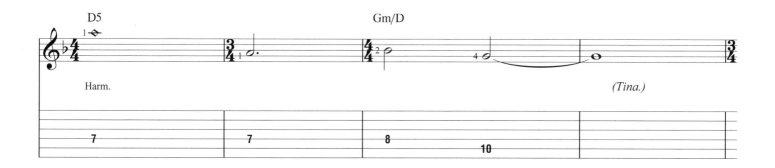

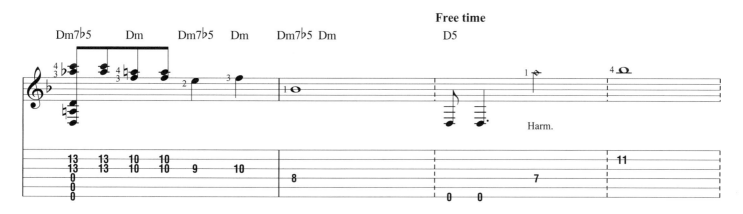

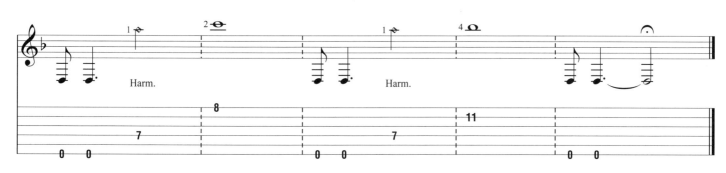

The Munsters Theme

from the Television Series
By Jack Marshall

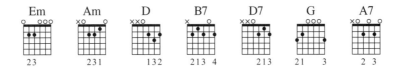

Strum Pattern: 2
Pick Pattern: 4

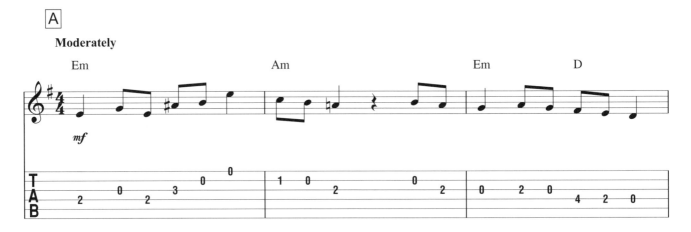

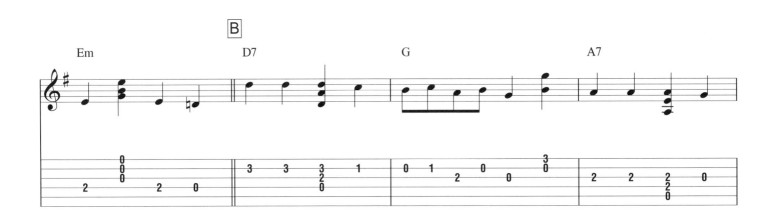

Copyright © 1973 SONGS OF UNIVERSAL, INC.
Copyright Renewed
All Rights Reserved   Used by Permission

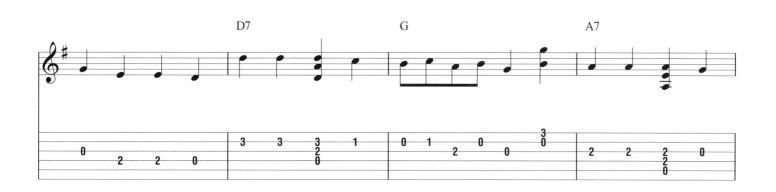

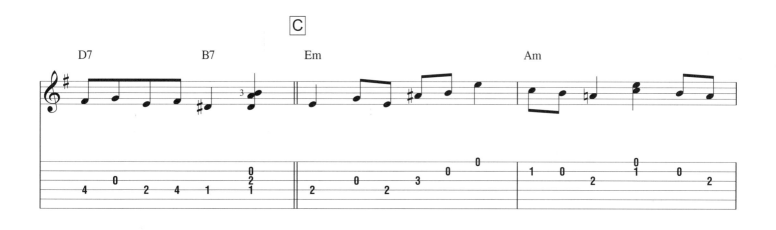

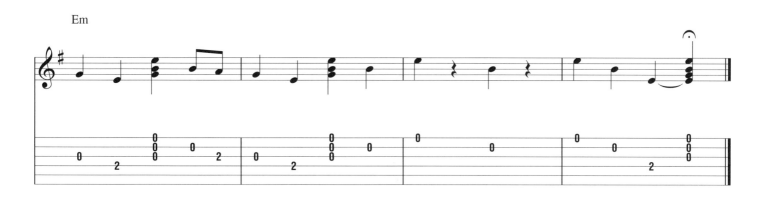

The Outer Limits

from the MGM Television Production OUTER LIMITS

By Nicholas Pike

Copyright © 1999 U/A Music Inc.
All Rights Administered by Sony/ATV Music Publishing LLC, 424 Church Street, Suite 1200, Nashville, TN 37219
International Copyright Secured   All Rights Reserved

Pet Sematary

Words and Music by Douglas Colvin, John Cummings, Jeffrey Hyman and Daniel Rey

Strum Pattern: 2
Pick Pattern: 1

Intro
Moderately fast

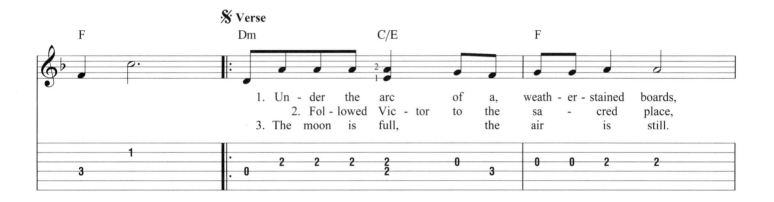

1. Un - der the arc of a, weath - er - stained boards,
2. Fol - lowed Vic - tor to the sa - cred place,
3. The moon is full, the air is still.

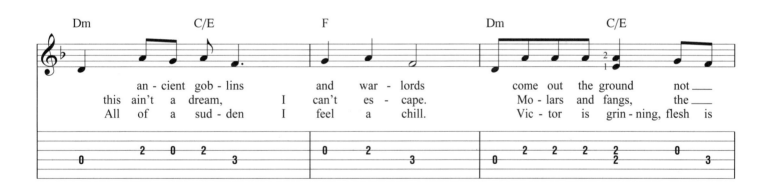

an - cient gob - lins and war - lords come out the ground not ___
this ain't a dream, I can't es - cape. Mo - lars and fangs, the ___
All of a sud - den I feel a chill. Vic - tor is grin - ning, flesh is

mak - in' a sound. The smell of death is ___ all a - round.
click - ing of bones, spir - its moan - ing a - mong the tomb - stones.
rot - ing a - way, skel - e - tons dance, I curse this day.

© 1989 WARNER-TAMERLANE PUBLISHING CORP., RABINOWITZ MUSIC and TACO TUNES
All Rights for RABINOWITZ MUSIC Administered by WARNER-TAMERLANE PUBLISHING CORP.
All Rights Reserved   Used by Permission

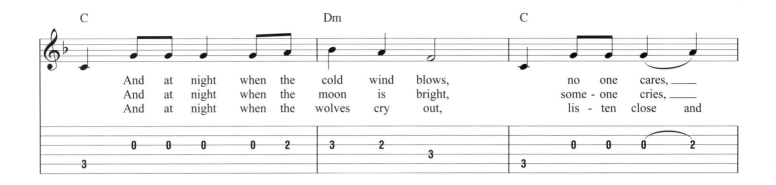

And at night when the cold wind blows, no one cares, _____
And at night when the moon is bright, some - one cries, _____
And at night when the wolves cry out, lis - ten close and

no - bod - y knows. _____
some - thing ain't right. _____
you can hear me shout. _____

Chorus

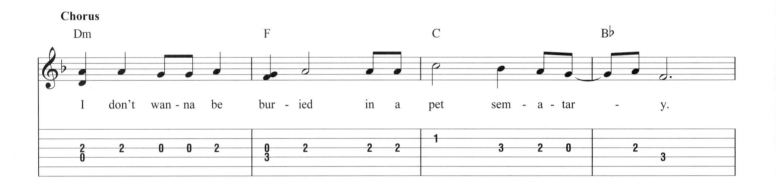

I don't wan - na be bur - ied in a pet sem - a - tar - y.

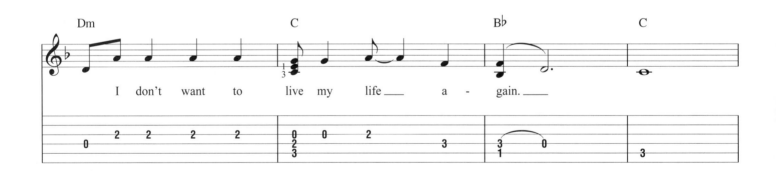

I don't want to live my life _____ a - gain. _____

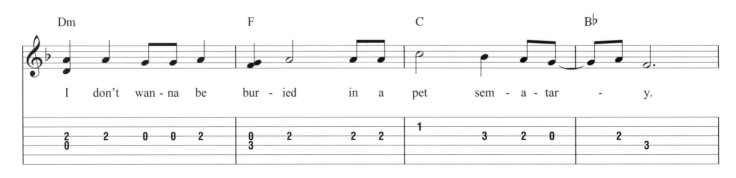

I don't wan - na be bur - ied in a pet sem - a - tar - y.

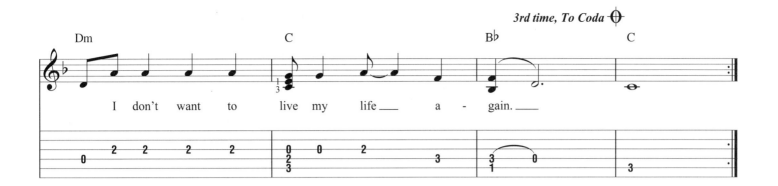

Interlude

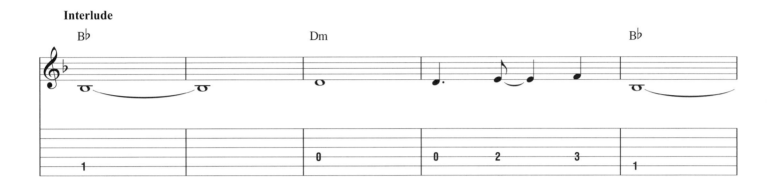

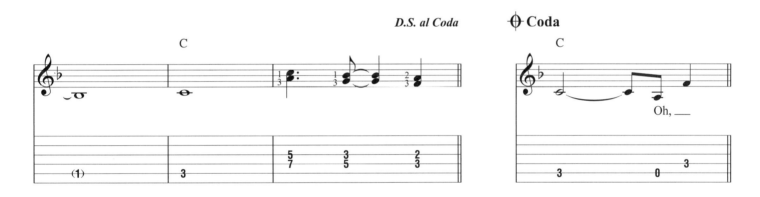

Outro

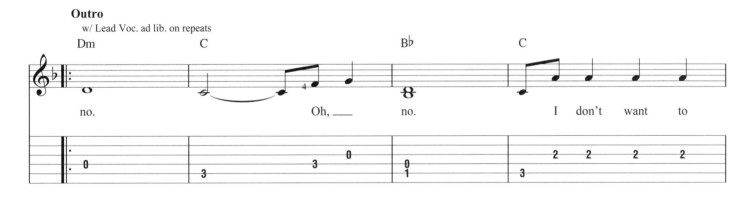

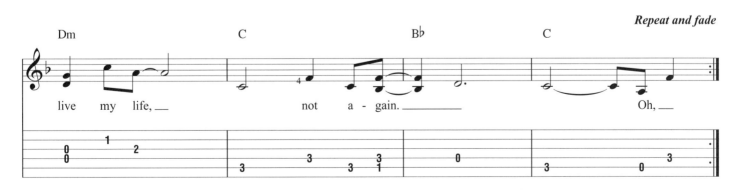

The Phantom of the Opera

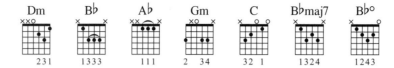

from THE PHANTOM OF THE OPERA
Music by Andrew Lloyd Webber
Lyrics by Charles Hart
Additional Lyrics by Richard Stilgoe and Mike Batt

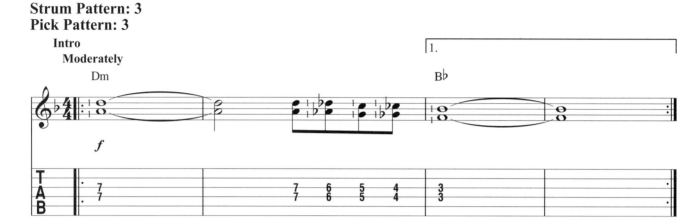

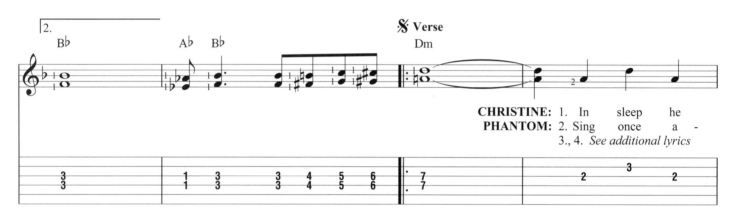

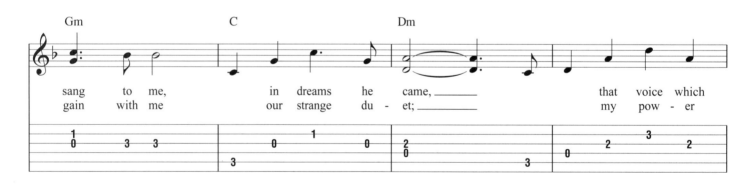

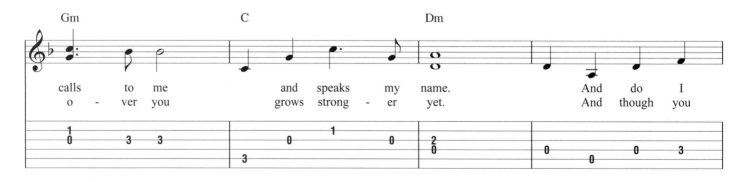

© Copyright 1986 Andrew Lloyd Webber licensed to The Really Useful Group Ltd.
International Copyright Secured   All Rights Reserved

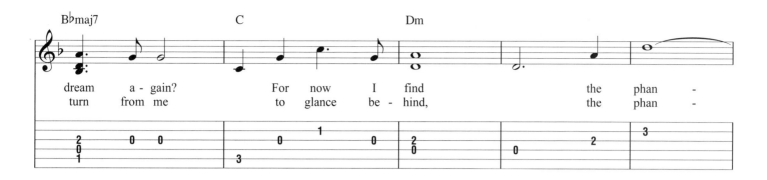

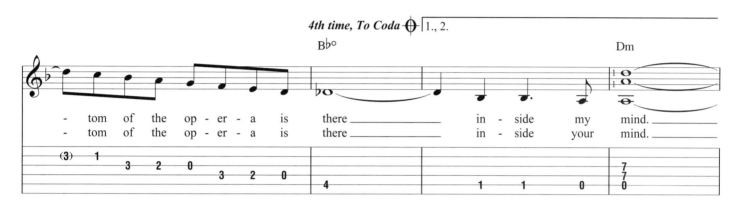

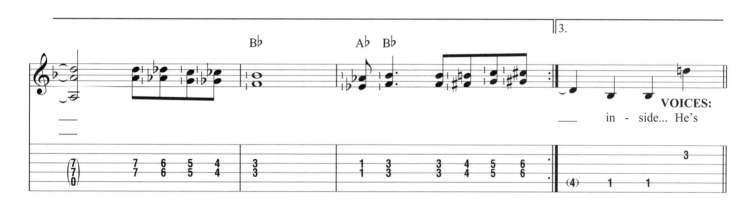

Interlude

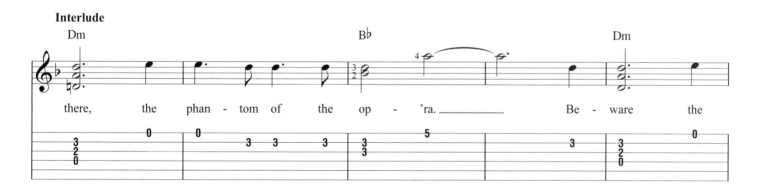

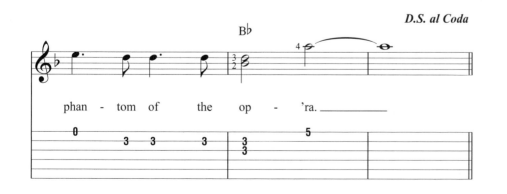

Outro

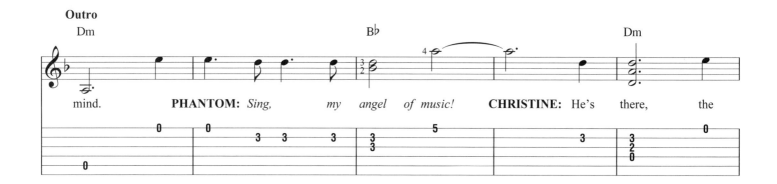

mind.   **PHANTOM:** *Sing,   my   angel   of   music!*   **CHRISTINE:** He's   there,   the

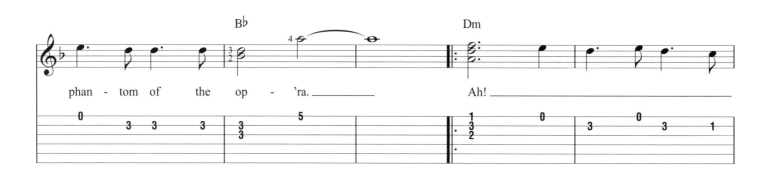

phan - tom   of   the   op - 'ra. _____   Ah! _____

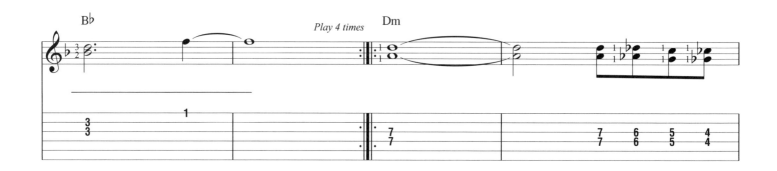

Play 4 times

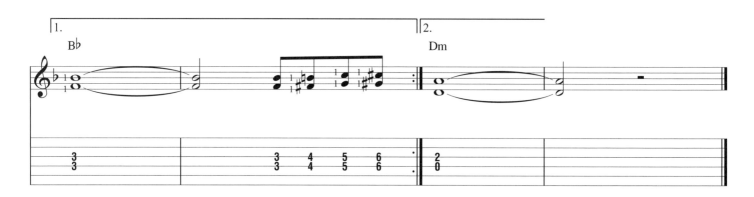

Additional Lyrics

CHRISTINE: 3. Those who have seen your face
           Draw back in fear.
           I am the mask you wear.
PHANTOM: It's me they hear.
    BOTH: {Your / My} spirit and {my / your} voice in one combined;
           The phantom of the opera is there inside...

PHANTOM: 4. In all your fantasies,
           You always knew
           That man and mystery
CHRISTINE: Were both in you.
    BOTH: And in this labyrinth where night is blind,
           The phantom of the opera is {here / there}
           Inside {my / your} mind.

(Ghost) Riders in the Sky

(A Cowboy Legend)

from RIDERS IN THE SKY

By Stan Jones

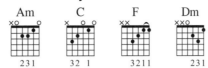

*Capo I

Strum Pattern: 1, 3
Pick Pattern: 1, 3

Intro
Moderately, in 2

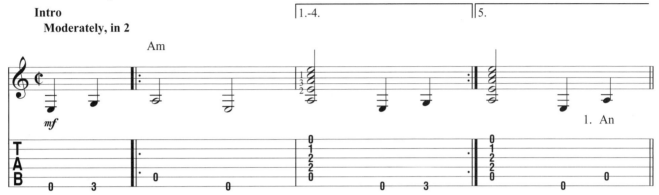

*Optional: To match recording, place capo at 1st fret.

Verse

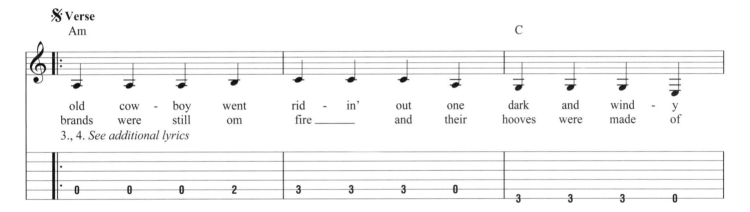

old cow-boy went rid-in' out one dark and wind-y
brands were still om fire _____ and their hooves were made of
3., 4. *See additional lyrics*

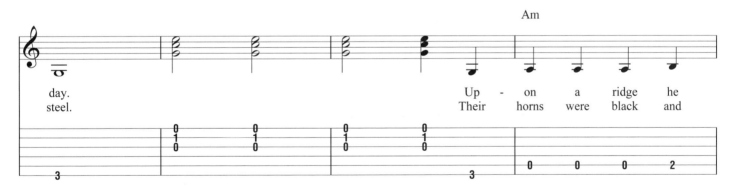

day.
steel.

Up - on a ridge he
Their horns were black and

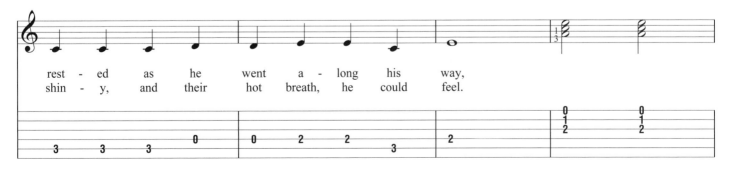

rest - ed as he went a - long his way,
shin - y, and their hot breath, he could feel.

© 1949 (Renewed) EDWIN H. MORRIS & COMPANY, A Division of MPL Music Publishing, Inc.
All Rights Reserved

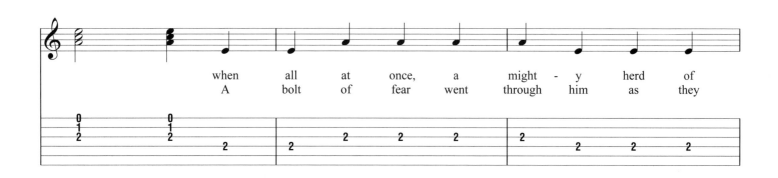

when all at once, a might - y herd of
A bolt of fear went through him as they

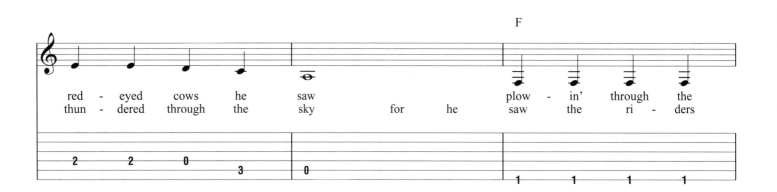

F

red - eyed cows he saw plow - in' through the
thun - dered through the sky for he saw the ri - ders

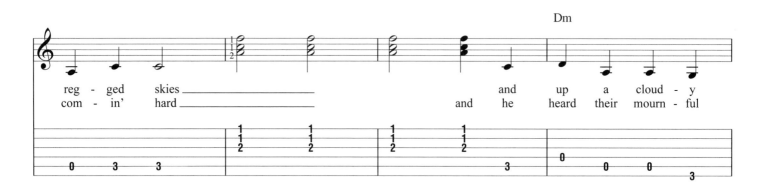

Dm

reg - ged skies _____ and up a cloud - y
com - in' hard _____ and he heard their mourn - ful

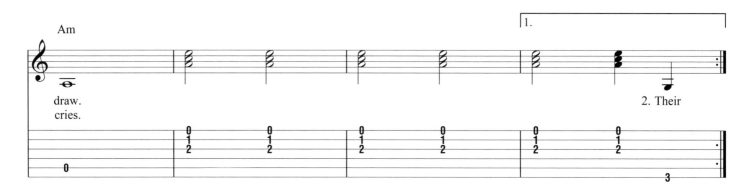

Am

1.

draw.
cries.
2. Their

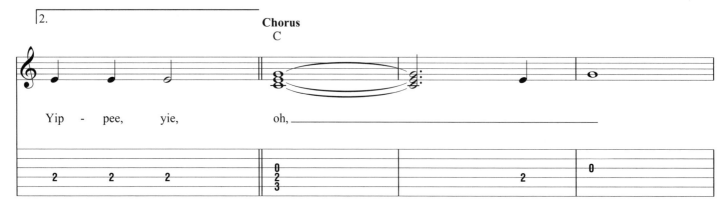

2.

Chorus
C

Yip - pee, yie, oh, _____

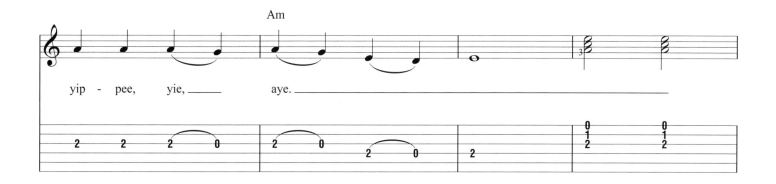

yip - pee, yie, _____ aye. _____

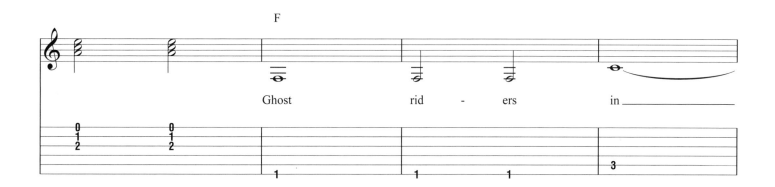

Ghost rid - ers in _____

To Coda

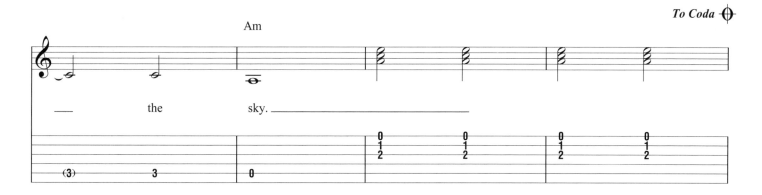

____ the sky. _____

Interlude

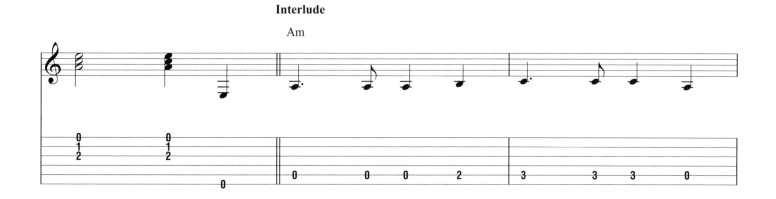

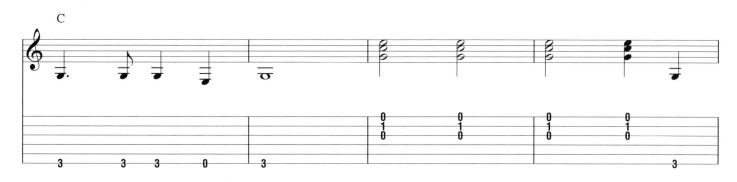

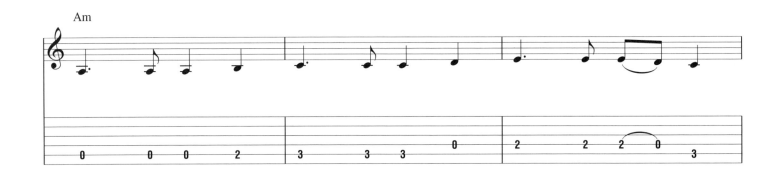

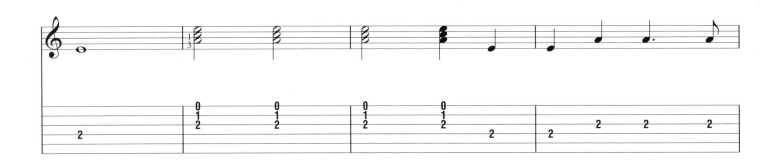

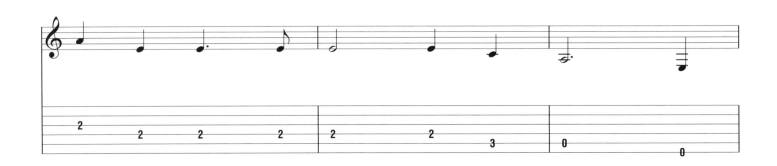

D.S. al Coda
(take repeat)

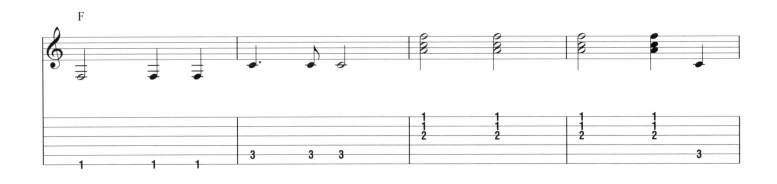

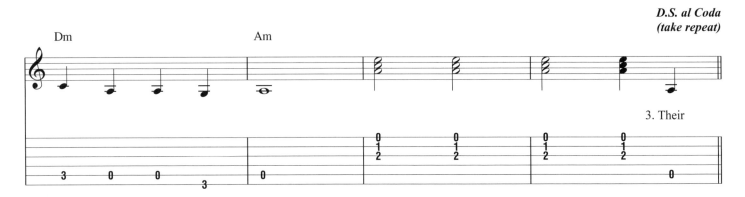

3. Their

Coda

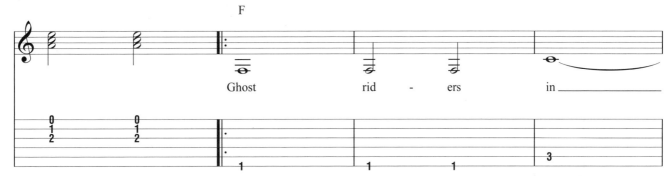

Ghost   rid - ers   in

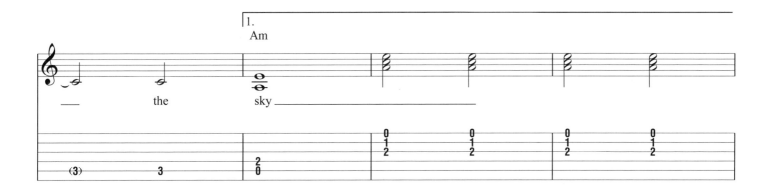

1.

the   sky

2.

sky.

Additional Lyrics

3. Their faces gaunt, their eyes are blurred, their shirts all soaked with sweat.
   He's ridin' hard to carch that herd, but ain't caught 'em yet
   'Cause they've got to ride forever on that range up in the sky
   On horses snortin' fire. As they ride on, hear their cry.

4. As the riders loped on by him, he heard one call his name,
   "If you want to save your soul from Hell a ridin' on our range,
   Then, cowboy, change your ways today, or with us you will ride,
   Tryin' to catch the Devil's herd across these endless skies."

Purple People Eater™

Words and Music by Sheb Wooley ®

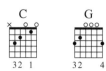

Strum Pattern: 2
Pick Pattern: 1

Intro
Moderately slow, in 2

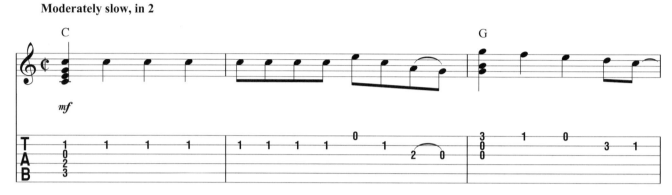

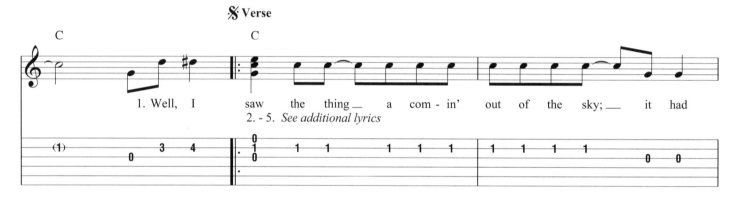

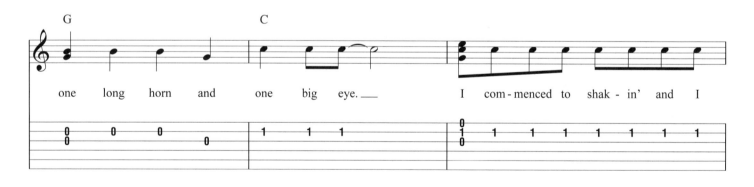

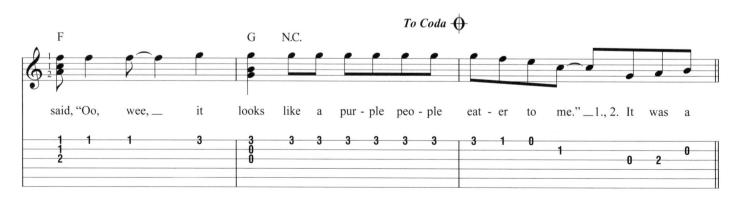

Copyright © 1958 by CORDIAL MUSIC CO.
Copyright Renewed 1986 by CHANNEL MUSIC CO.
International Copyright Secured   All Rights Reserved including character

Chorus

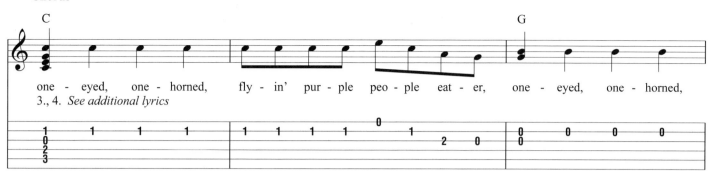

one - eyed, one - horned, fly - in' pur - ple peo - ple eat - er, one - eyed, one - horned,
3., 4. *See additional lyrics*

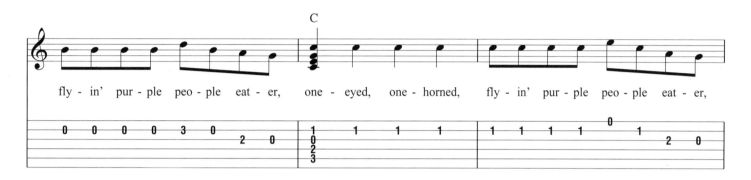

fly - in' pur - ple peo - ple eat - er, one - eyed, one - horned, fly - in' pur - ple peo - ple eat - er,

1., 2., 3.   **4.**   *D.S. al Coda*

sure looked strange to me. _____   2. Well, then he   5. Well, then he

⊕ Coda

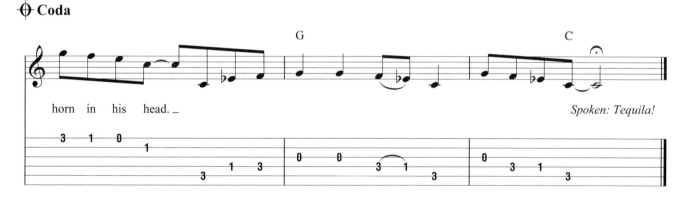

horn in his head. _   *Spoken: Tequila!*

Additional Lyrics

2. Well, then he came down to earth and he lit in a tree.
   I said, "Mister purple people eater, don't eat me."
   I heard him say in a voice so gruff,
Spoken: "I wouldn't eat you 'cause you're so tough."

3. I said, "Mister purple people eater, what's your line?"
   He said, "Eatin' purple people, and it sure is fine,
   But that's not the reason that I came to land,
Spoken: I wanna get a job in a rock and roll band."

Chorus 3 Well, bless my soul, rock 'n' roll, flyin' purple people eater,
   Pigeon-toed, under-growed, flyin' purple people eater,
   He wears short shorts, friendly little people eater.
   What a sight to see.

4. And then he swung from the tree and he lit on the ground,
   And he started to rock, a really rockin' around.
   A crazy ditty with a swingin' tune,
   Singin' *Spoken: bop, bap a loop a lap a loom, bam, boom.*

Chorus 4 Well, bless my soul, rock 'n' roll, flyin' purple people eater,
   Pigeon-toed, under-growed, flyin' purple people eater,
Spoken: "I like short shorts!" friendly little people eater.
   What a sight to see.

5. Well, then he went on his way and then a what do you know,
   I saw him last night on the Star Out show.
   He was blowin' it out, really knockin' 'em dead,
   Playin' rock 'n' roll music thru the horn in his head.

The Simpsons™ Halloween Special Main Title Theme

from the Twentieth Century Fox Television Series THE SIMPSONS

By Danny Elfman

Strum Pattern: 6
Pick Pattern: 1

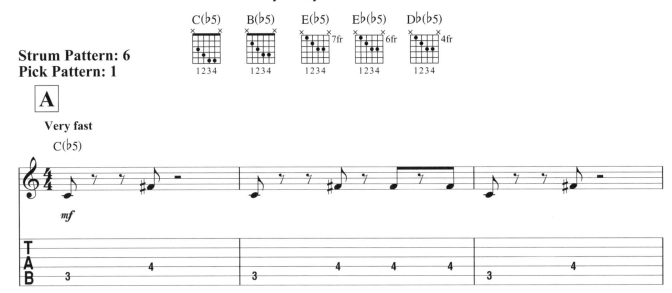

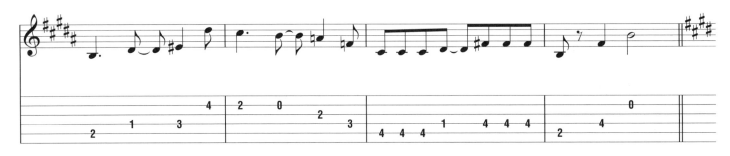

Copyright © 1990, 1991 Fox Film Music Corporation
All Rights Reserved   Used by Permission

Song of the Volga Boatman

Russian Folk Song

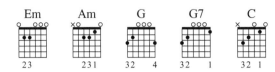

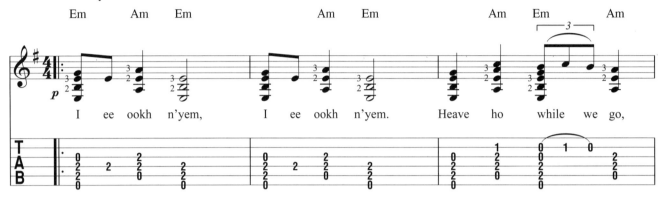

Strum Pattern: 4
Pick Pattern: 1

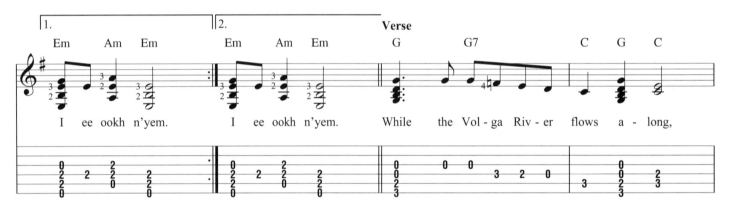

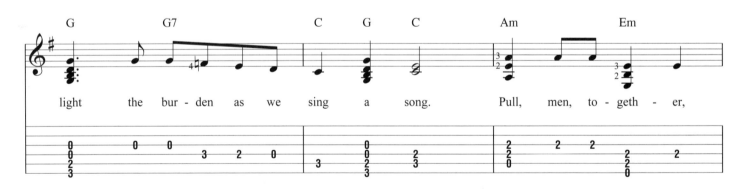

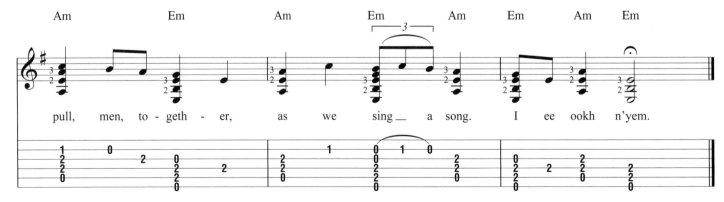

Copyright © 2015 by HAL LEONARD CORPORATION
International Copyright Secured   All Rights Reserved

Tales from the Crypt Theme

By Danny Elfman

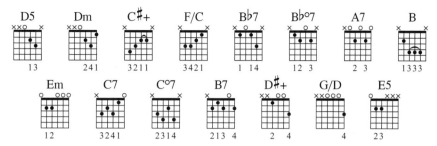

Strum Pattern: 5
Pick Pattern: 5

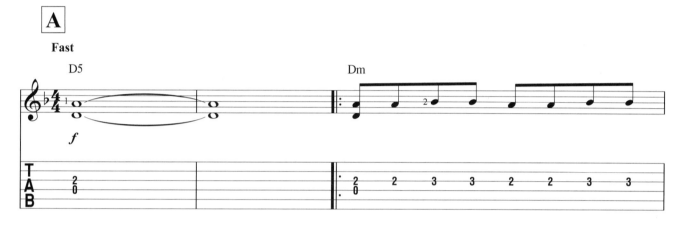

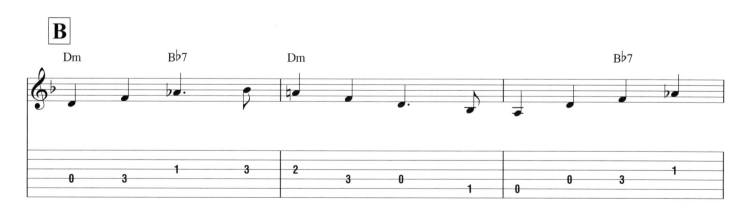

Copyright © 1989 Songs Crypt
All Rights Administered by Sony/ATV Music Publishing LLC, 424 Church Street, Suite 1200, Nashville, TN 37219
International Copyright Secured   All Rights Reserved

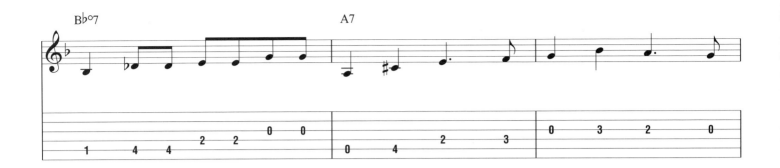

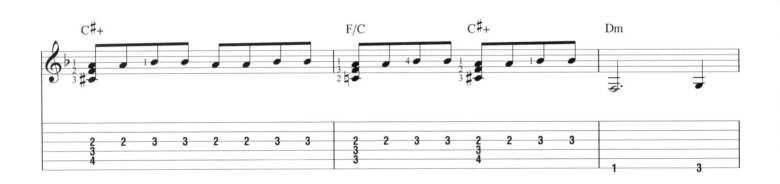

C

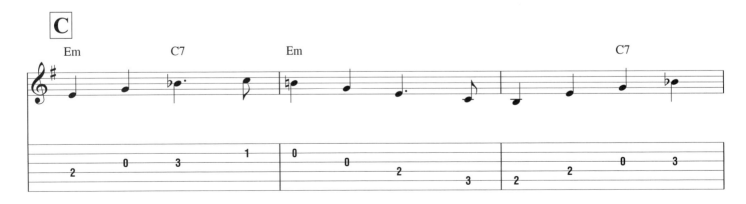

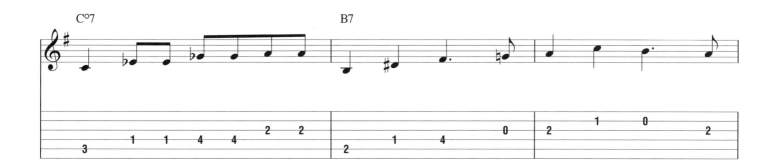

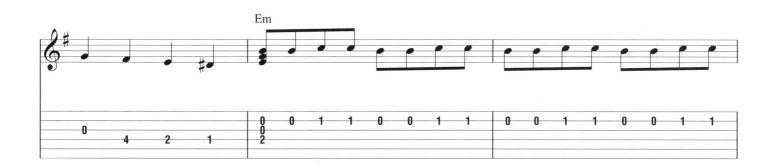

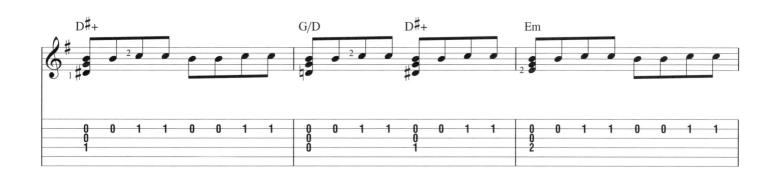

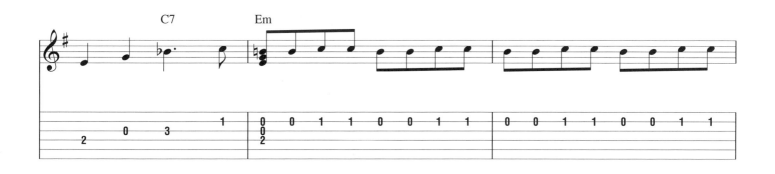

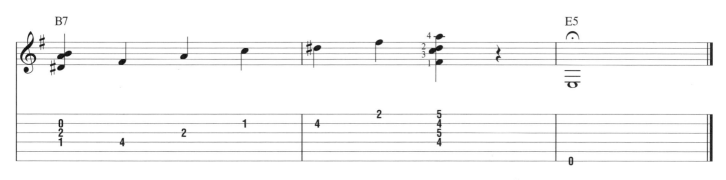

Spooky

Words and Music by J.R. Cobb, Buddy Buie, Harry Middlebrooks and Mike Shapiro

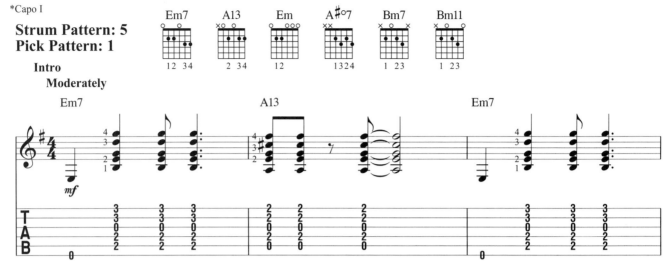

*Capo I

Strum Pattern: 5
Pick Pattern: 1

Intro
Moderately

*Optional: To match recording, place capo at 1st fret.

𝄋 **Verse**

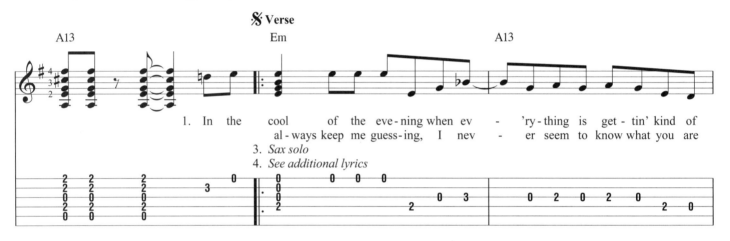

1. In the cool of the eve-ning when ev-'ry-thing is get-tin' kind of
   al-ways keep me guess-ing, I nev-er seem to know what you are
3. *Sax solo*
4. *See additional lyrics*

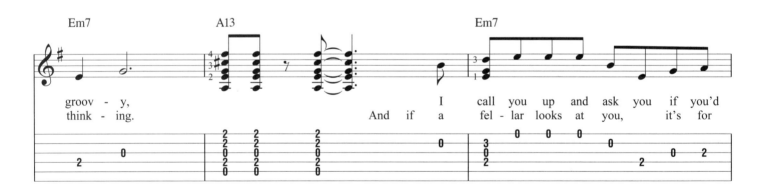

groov - y,
think - ing.
And if a
I call you up and ask you if you'd
fel-lar looks at you, it's for

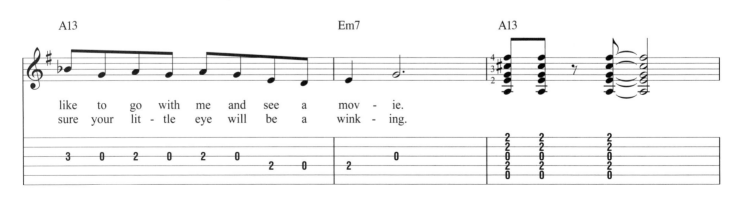

like to go with me and see a mov - ie.
sure your lit - tle eye will be a wink - ing.

Copyright © 1965 Sony/ATV Music Publishing LLC
Copyright Renewed
All Rights Administered by Sony/ATV Music Publishing LLC, 424 Church Street, Suite 1200, Nashville, TN 37219
International Copyright Secured   All Rights Reserved

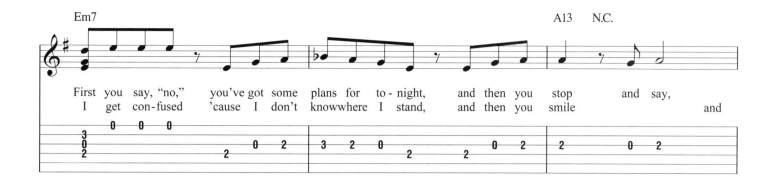

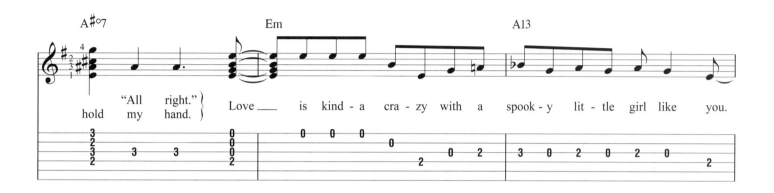

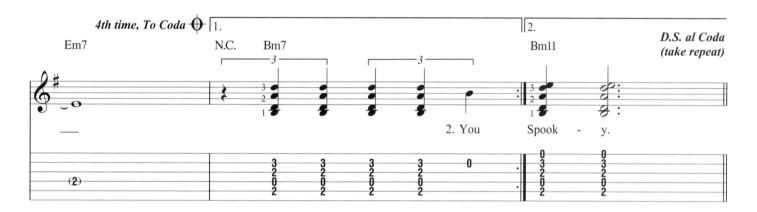

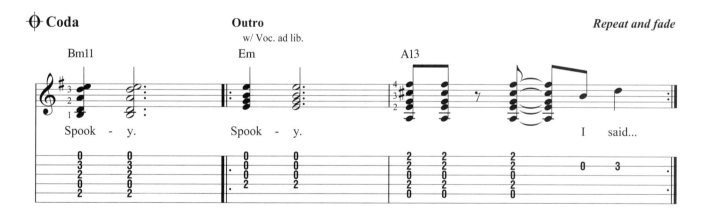

Additional Lyrics

4. If you decide some day to stop this little game that you are playing,
I'm gonna tell you all the things my heart's been a dying to be saying.
Just like a ghost, you've been a haunting my dreams,
So I'll propose on Halloween.
Love is kinda crazy with a spooky little girl like you. Spooky.

Superstition

Words and Music by Stevie Wonder

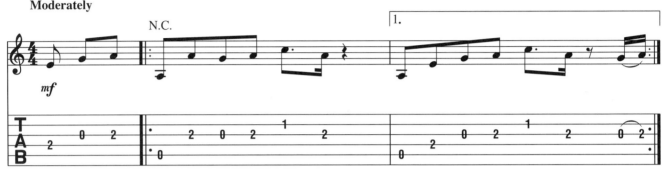

Strum Pattern: 5
Pick Pattern: 1

Intro
Moderately

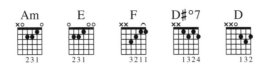

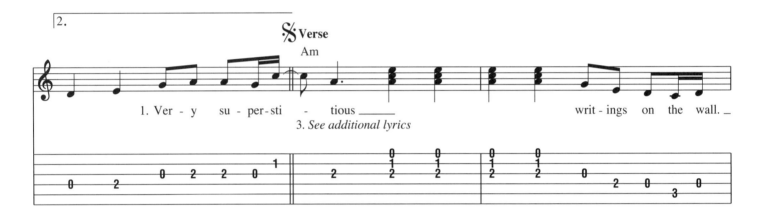

1. Ver - y su - per - sti - tious _____

3. *See additional lyrics*

writ - ings on the wall. _

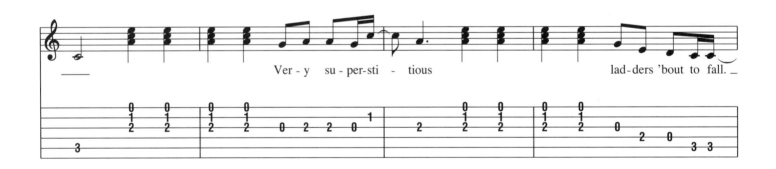

Ver - y su - per - sti - tious

lad - ders 'bout to fall. _

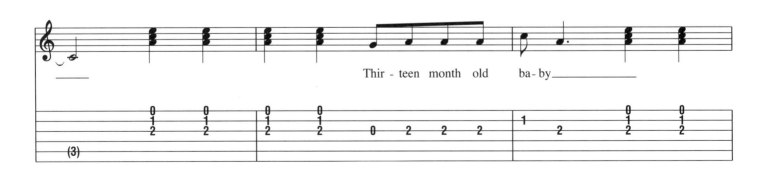

Thir - teen month old ba - by _____

© 1972 (Renewed 2000) JOBETE MUSIC CO., INC. and BLACK BULL MUSIC
c/o EMI APRIL MUSIC INC.
All Rights Reserved   International Copyright Secured   Used by Permission

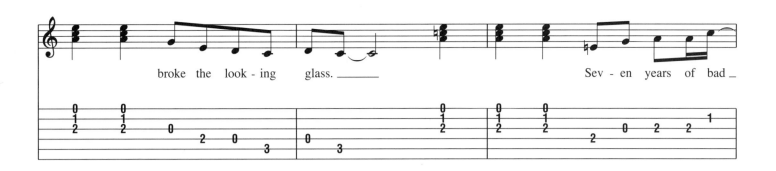

broke the look - ing glass. _____ Sev - en years of bad _

_____ luck, _____ the good things in your past. _

Chorus

E   F   E   D#°7

When you be - lieve ___ in things that you don't un - der - stand ___ then you suf - fer. _

To Coda ⊕

D   E   N.C.   Am

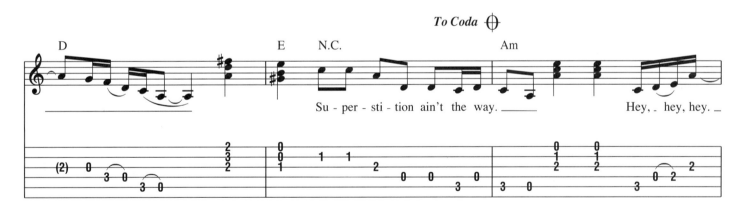

Su - per - sti - tion ain't the way. _____ Hey, _ hey, hey. _

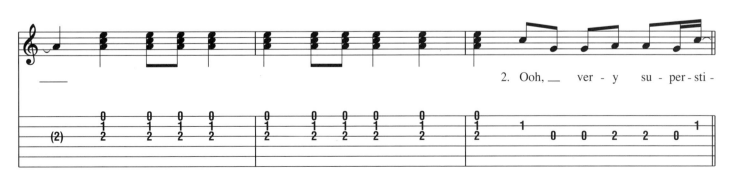

_____ 2. Ooh, ___ ver - y su - per - sti -

Verse

-tious, _____ wash your face and hands. _

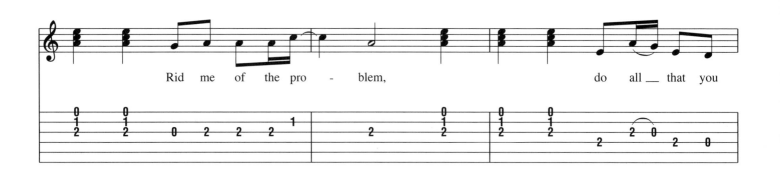

Rid me of the pro - blem, do all _ that you

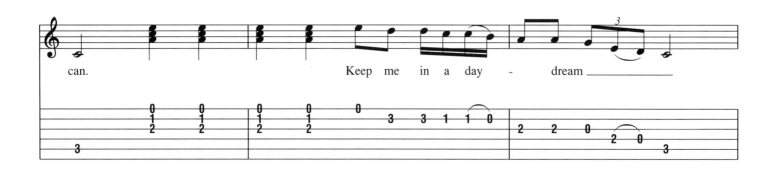

can. Keep me in a day - dream _____

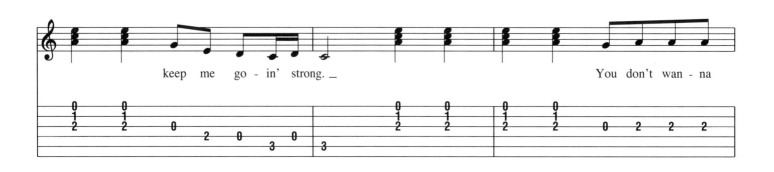

keep me go - in' strong. _ You don't wan - na

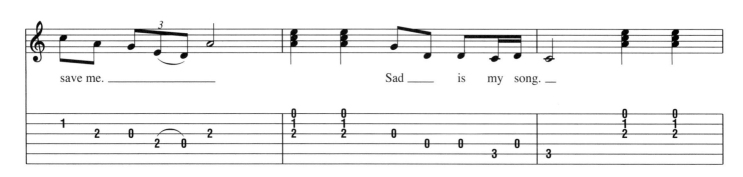

save me. _____ Sad _ is my song. _

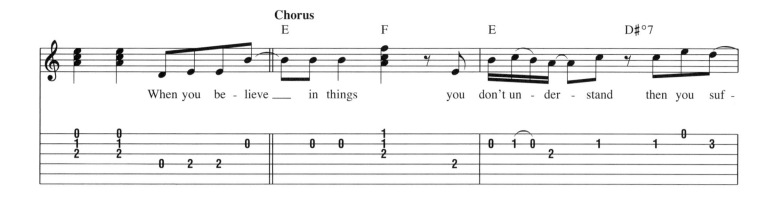

Chorus

When you be - lieve ___ in things you don't un - der - stand then you suf -

- fer. ___ Su - per - sti - tion ___ ain't the way, ___ hey, ___

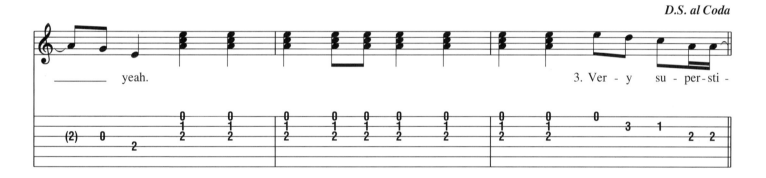

D.S. al Coda

___ yeah. 3. Ver - y su - per - sti -

Coda

Outro

Repeat and fade

Additional Lyrics

3. Very superstitious, nothing more to say.
Very superstitious, the devil's on his way.
Thirteen month old baby broke the looking glass.
Seven years of bad luck, the good things in your past.

The Thing

Words and Music by Charles R. Grean

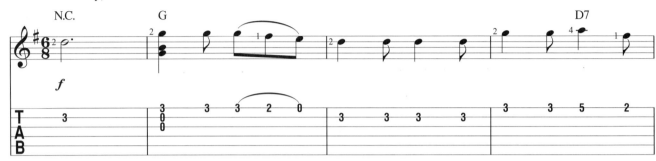

Strum Pattern: 8
Pick Pattern: 8

Intro
Moderately, in 2

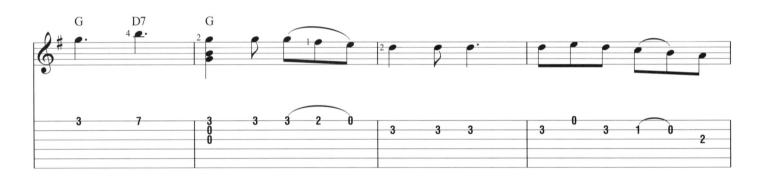

1. While

Verse

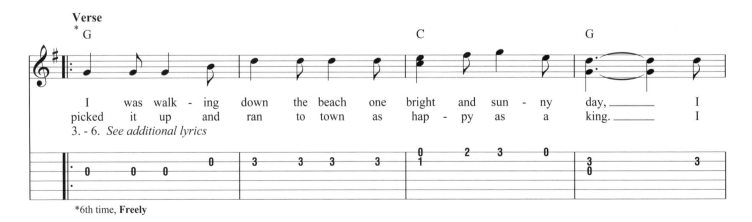

I was walk-ing down the beach one bright and sun-ny day,___ I
picked it up and ran to town as hap-py as a king.___ I

3. - 6. See additional lyrics

*6th time, **Freely***

Copyright © 1950 (Renewed) by Grean Music
All Rights Administered for the U.S.A. by September Music Corporation
International Copyright Secured   All Rights Reserved

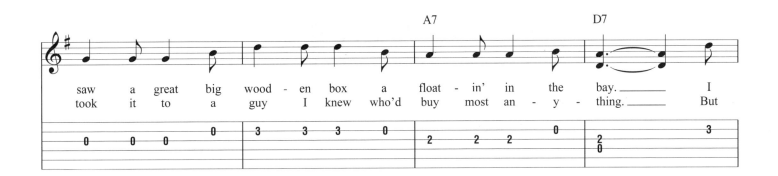

saw a great big wood - en box a float - in' in the bay. _____ I
took it to a guy I knew who'd buy most an - y - thing. _____ But

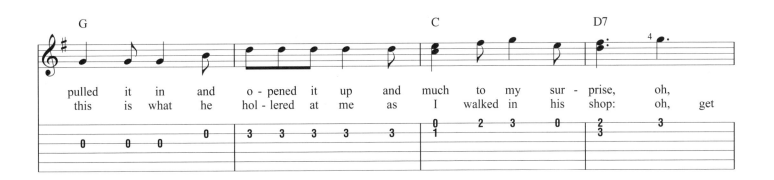

pulled it in and o - pened it up and much to my sur - prise, oh,
this is what he hol - lered at me as I walked in his shop: oh, get

I dis - cov - ered a...   right be - fore my eyes. Oh,
out of here with that...   be - fore I call a cop. Oh, get

*6th time, **A tempo**

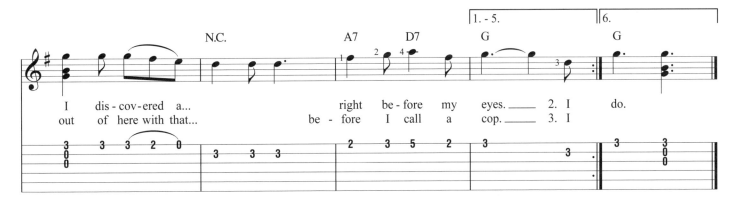

I dis - cov - ered a...   right be - fore my eyes. _____ 2. I do.
out of here with that...   be - fore I call a cop. _____ 3. I

Additional Lyrics

3. I turned around and got right out a runnin' for my life,
And then I took it home with me to give it to my wife.
But this is what she hollered at me as I walked in the door:
Oh, get out of here with that... and don't come back no more.
Oh, get out of here with that... and don't come back no more.

4. I wandered all around the town until I chanced to meet
A hobo who was looking for a handout on the street.
He said he'd take most any old thing, he was a desperate man,
But when I showed him the... he turned around and ran.
Oh, when I showed him the... he turned around and ran.

5. I wandered on for many years, a victim of my fate,
Until one day I came upon Saint Peter at the gate.
And when I tried to take it inside he told me where to go:
Get out of here with that... and take it down below.
Oh, get out of here with that... and take it down below.

6. The moral of the story is if you're out on the beach
And you should see a great big box and it's within your reach,
Don't ever stop and open it up, that's my advice to you,
'Cause you'll never get rid of the... no matter what you do.
Oh, you'll never get rid of the... no matter what you do.

This Is Halloween

from Tim Burton's THE NIGHTMARE BEFORE CHRISTMAS
Music and Lyrics by Danny Elfman

*Strum Pattern: 3
*Pick Pattern: 3

*Use Pattern 7 for ¾ meas.
Use Pattern 10 for ²⁄₄ meas.

© 1993 Buena Vista Music Company
All Rights Reserved   Used by Permission

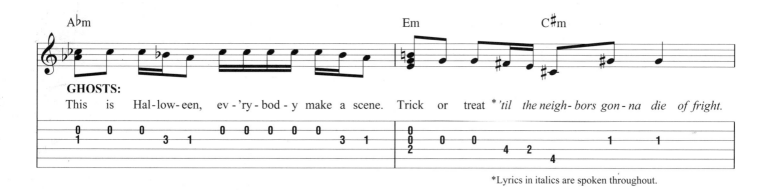

GHOSTS:
This is Hal-low-een, ev-'ry-bod-y make a scene. Trick or treat *'til the neigh-bors gon-na die of fright.

*Lyrics in italics are spoken throughout.

It's our town. Ev-'ry-bod-y scream in this town of Hal-low-

Verse

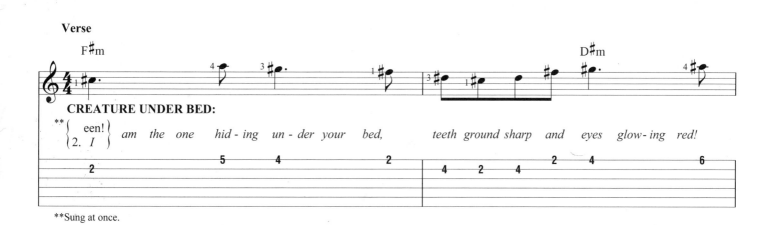

CREATURE UNDER BED:
** een! / 2. I am the one hid-ing un-der your bed, teeth ground sharp and eyes glow-ing red!

**Sung at once.

MAN UNDER THE STAIRS:
I am the one hid-ing un-der your stairs, fin-gers like snakes and spi-ders in my hair!

Chorus

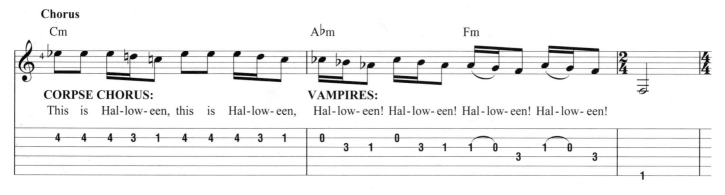

CORPSE CHORUS:
This is Hal-low-een, this is Hal-low-een,

VAMPIRES:
Hal-low-een! Hal-low-een! Hal-low-een! Hal-low-een!

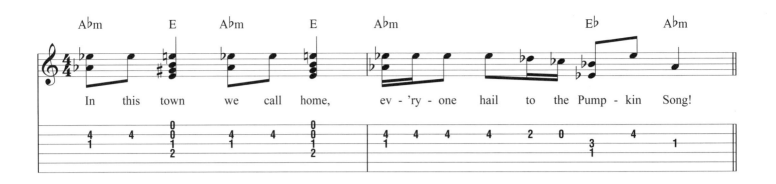

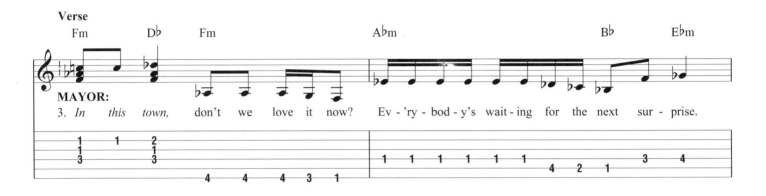

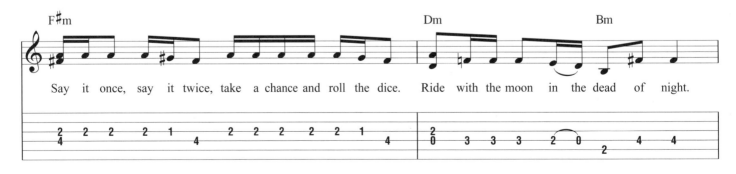

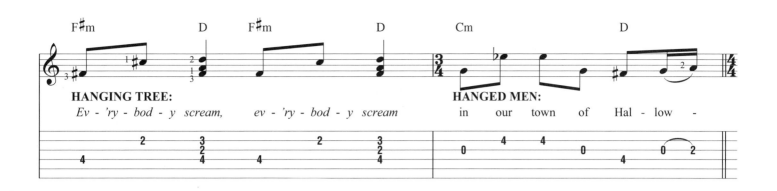

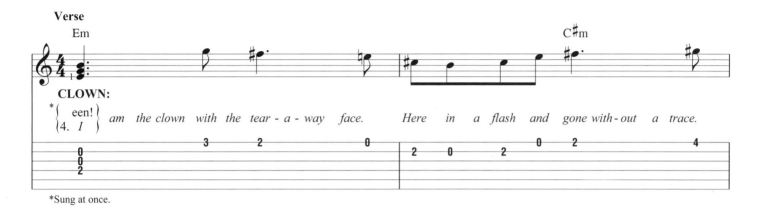

*Sung at once.

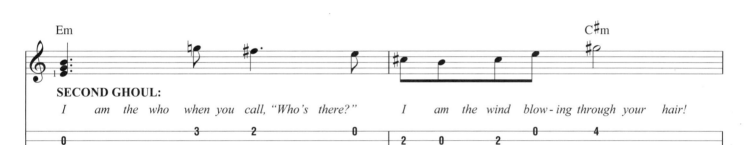

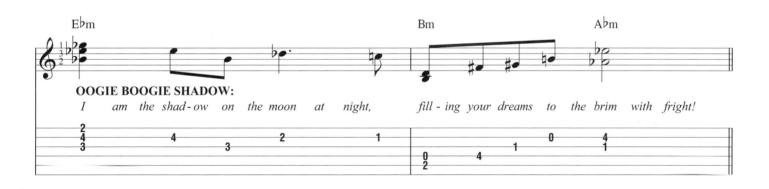

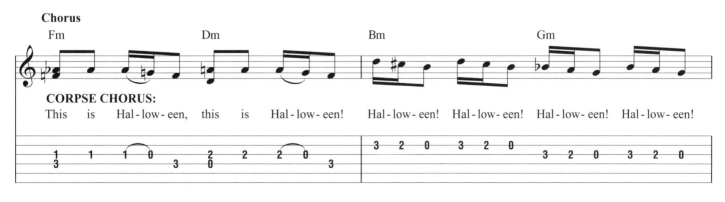

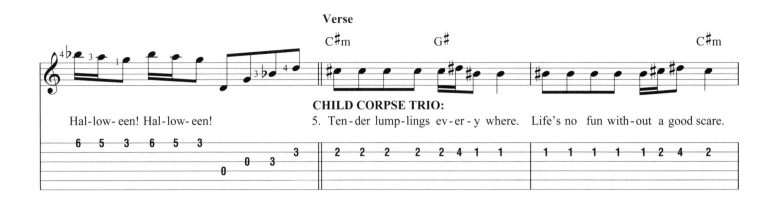

Verse

CHILD CORPSE TRIO:

Hal-low-een! Hal-low-een! 5. Ten-der lump-lings ev-er-y where. Life's no fun with-out a good scare.

PARENT CORPSES:

That's our job, but we're not ___ mean in our town ___ of Hal - low - een. ___

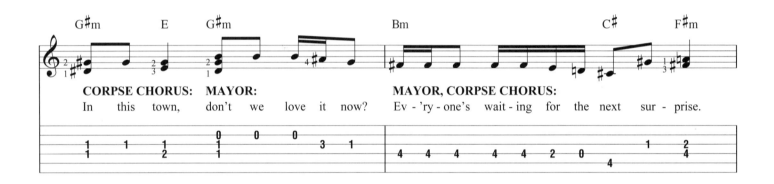

CORPSE CHORUS: MAYOR: **MAYOR, CORPSE CHORUS:**

In this town, don't we love it now? Ev -'ry-one's wait-ing for the next sur-prise.

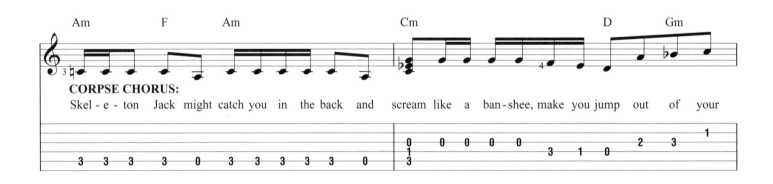

CORPSE CHORUS:

Skel - e - ton Jack might catch you in the back and scream like a ban-shee, make you jump out of your

skin! This is Hal-low-een, ev-'ry-bod - y scream! Won't ya please make way for a *ver - y spe-cial guy!*

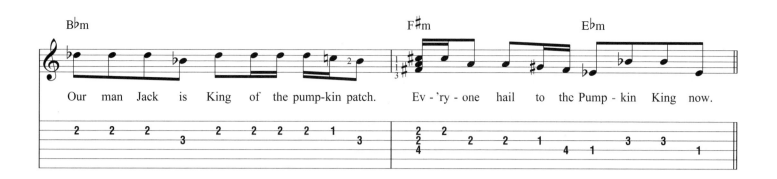

Our man Jack is King of the pump-kin patch. Ev-'ry-one hail to the Pump-kin King now.

Chorus

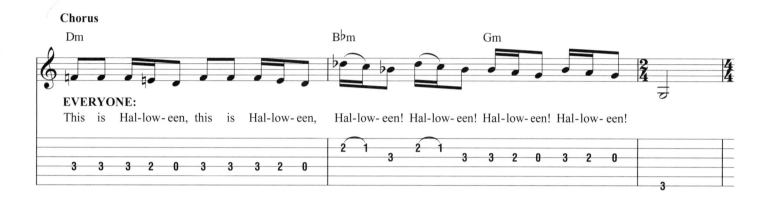

EVERYONE:
This is Hal-low-een, this is Hal-low-een, Hal-low-een! Hal-low-een! Hal-low-een! Hal-low-een!

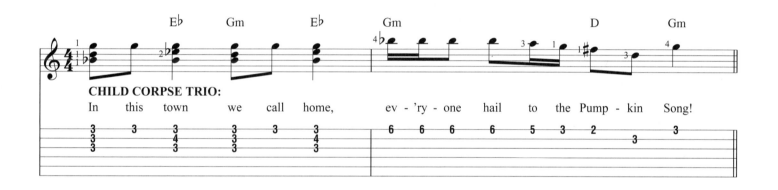

CHILD CORPSE TRIO:
In this town we call home, ev-'ry-one hail to the Pump-kin Song!

Outro

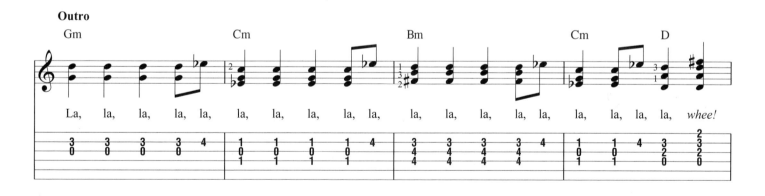

La, la, la, la, la, la, la, la, la, la, la, la, la, la, la, la, la, la, la, *whee!*

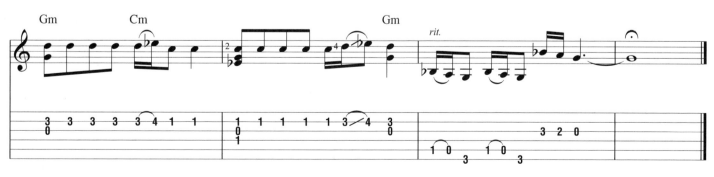

Thriller

Words and Music by Rod Temperton

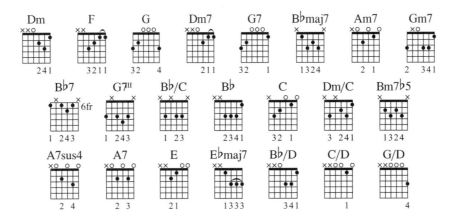

*Tune down 1/2 step:
(low to high) Eb-Ab-Db-Gb-Bb-Eb

Strum Pattern: 3
Pick Pattern: 3

Intro
Moderate Rock

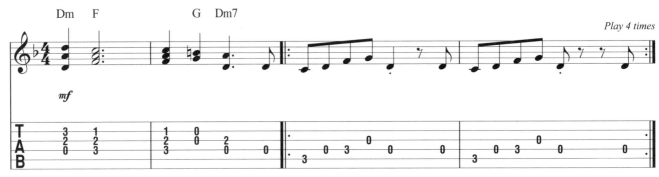

*Optional: To match recording, tune down 1/2 step.

𝄋 Verse

1. It's close to mid - night, __ and some - thin' e - vil's lurk - in' in the
2. You hear the door slam __ and re - al - ize there's no - where left to
3. They're out to get you. __ There's de - mons clos - in' in on ev - 'ry

**Sung as written.

Copyright © 1982 RODSONGS
All Rights Controlled and Administered by ALMO MUSIC CORP.
All Rights Reserved   Used by Permission

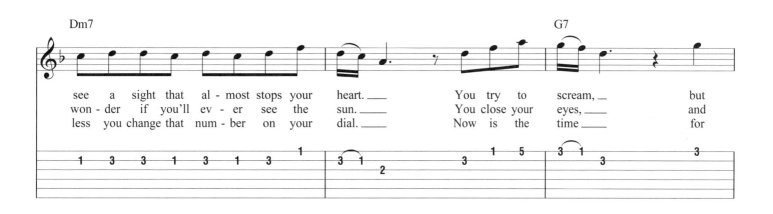

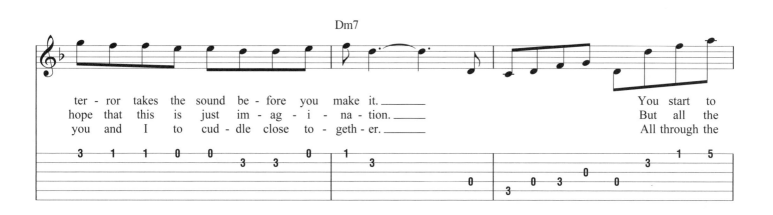

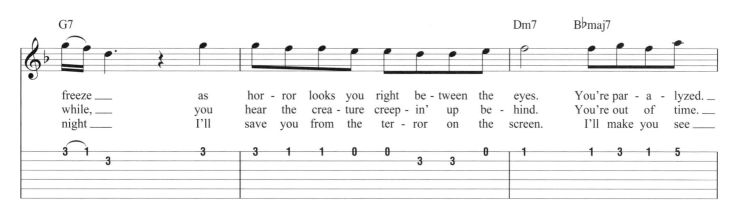

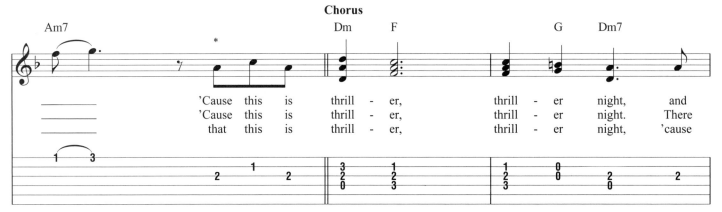

*Sung one octave higher.

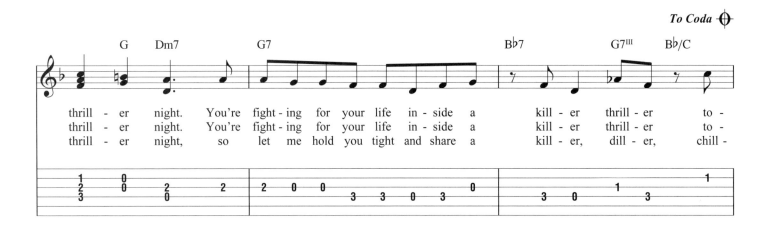

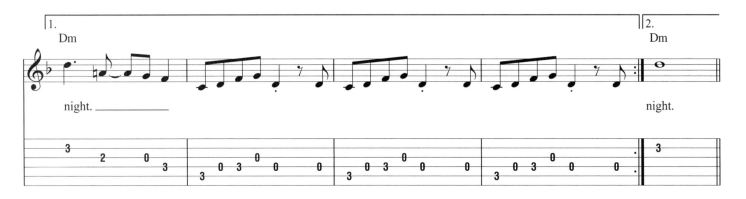

Bridge

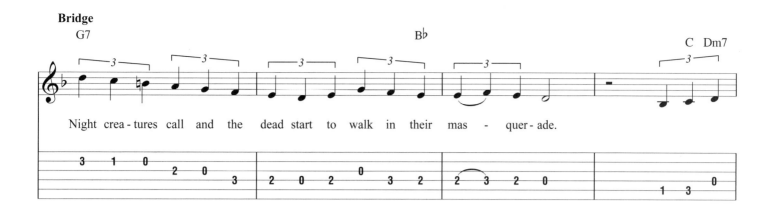

Night crea - tures call and the dead start to walk in their mas - quer - ade.

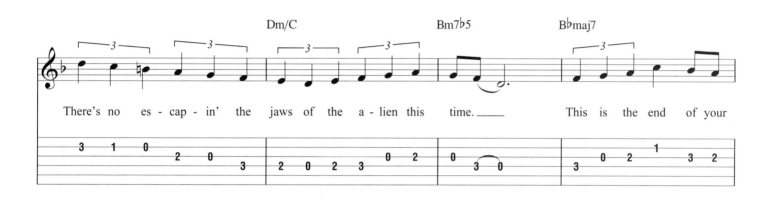

There's no es - cap - in' the jaws of the a - lien this time. _____ This is the end of your

D.S. al Coda   ⊕ **Coda**

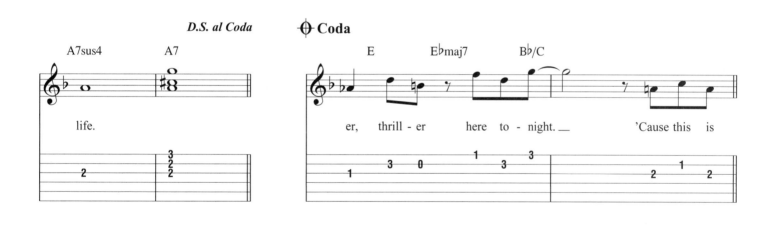

life.   er, thrill - er here to - night. __ 'Cause this is

Chorus

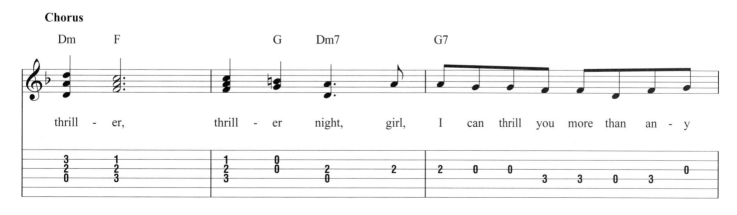

thrill - er, thrill - er night, girl, I can thrill you more than an - y

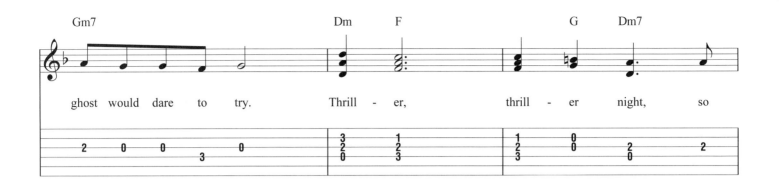

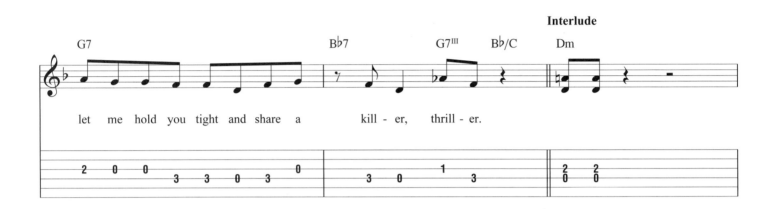

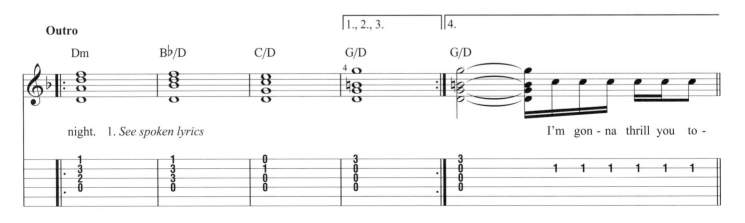

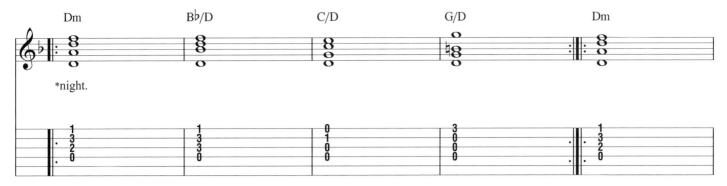

*night.

*Sung 1st time only.

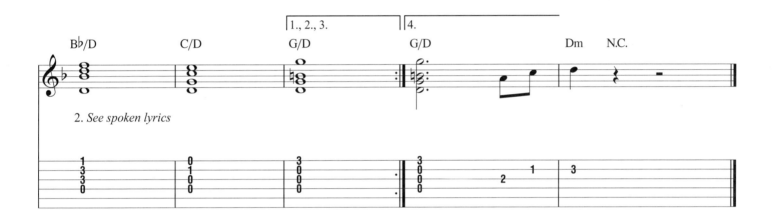

2. See spoken lyrics

Additional Lyrics

1. *Darkness falls across the land.*
   The midnight hour is close at hand.
   Creatures crawl in search of blood
   To terrorize y'all's neighborhood.
   And whosoever shall be found
   Without the soul for getting down
   Must stand and face the hounds of hell
   And rot inside a corpse's shell.

2. *The foulest stench is in the air,*
   The funk of forty thousand years,
   And grizzly ghouls from every tomb
   Are closing in to seal your doom.
   And though you fight to stay alive,
   Your body starts to shiver,
   For no mere mortal can resist
   The evil of the thriller.

Time Warp

from THE ROCKY HORROR PICTURE SHOW
Words and Music by Richard O'Brien

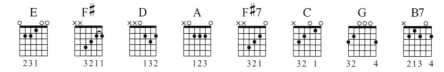

*Capo V

Strum Pattern: 5
Pick Pattern: 1

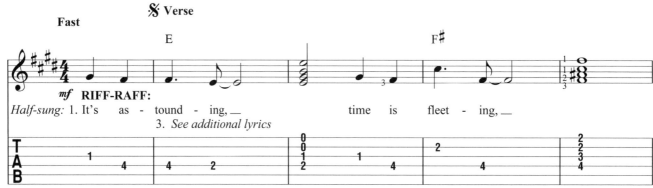

*Optional: To match recording, place capo at 5th fret.

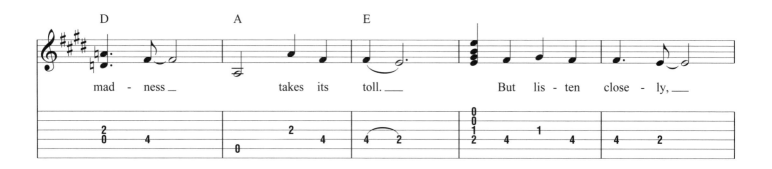

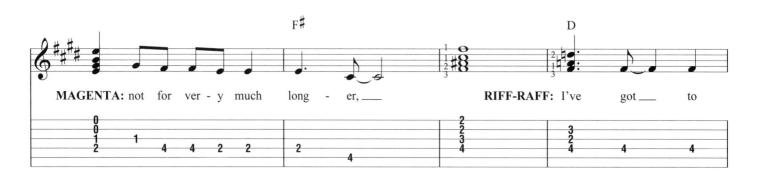

Copyright © 1974 (Renewed 2002) Druidcrest Music Ltd.
All Rights Administered by Wixen Music Publishing, Inc.
All Rights Reserved   Used by Permission

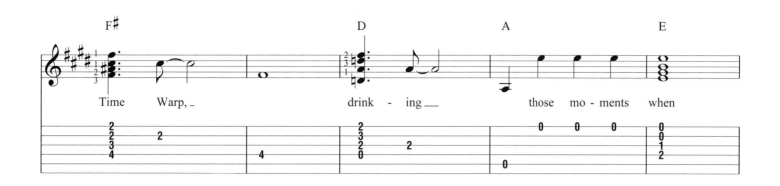

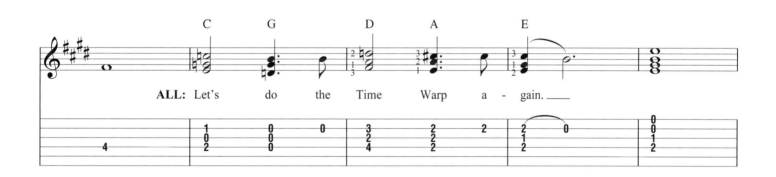

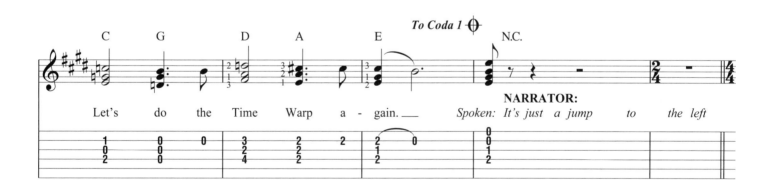

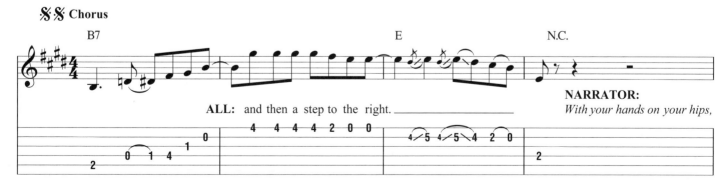

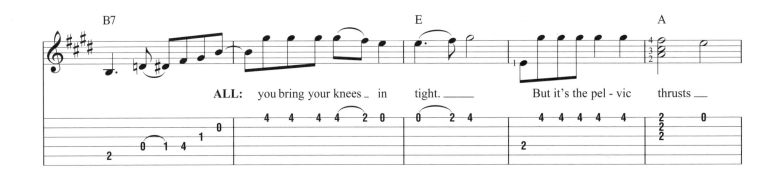

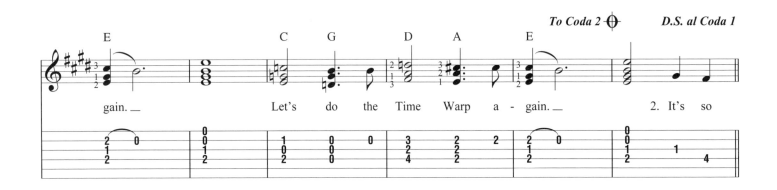

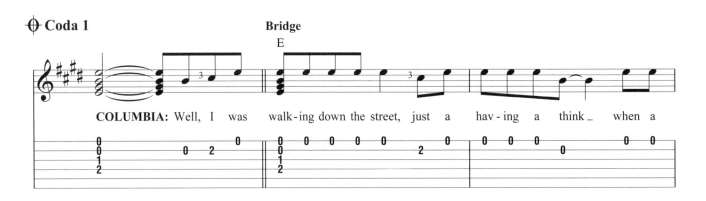

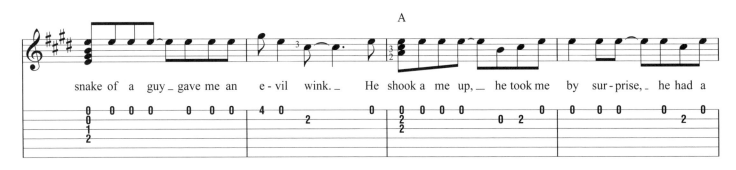

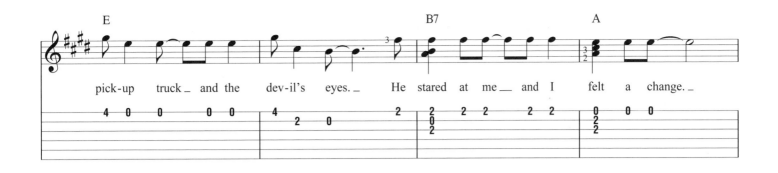

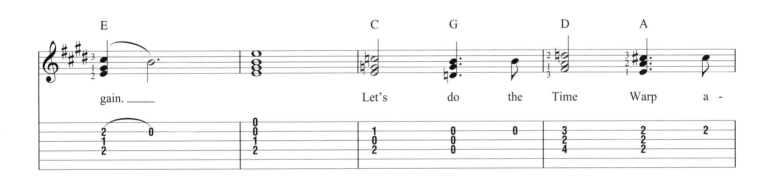

D.S.S. al Coda 2

Coda 2

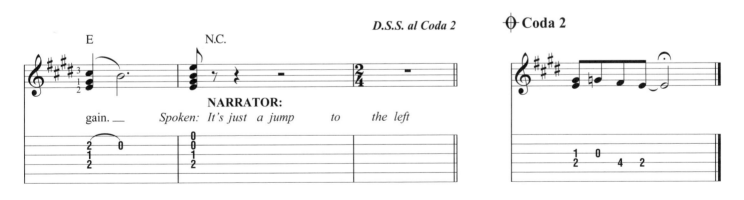

Additional Lyrics

MAGENTA: 3. It's so dreamy,
   Oh, fantasy, free me
   So you can't see me,
   No, not at all.
   In another dimension,
   With voyeuristic intention,
   Well secluded, I see all.

RIFF-RAFF: 4. With a bit of a mind flip
MAGENTA: You're into the time slip.
RIFF-RAFF: And nothing can ever be the same.
MAGENTA: You're spaced out on sensation
RIFF-RAFF: Like you're under sedation.
ALL: Let's do the Time Warp again.
   Let's do the Time Warp again.

Toccata and Fugue in D Minor

By Johann Sebastian Bach

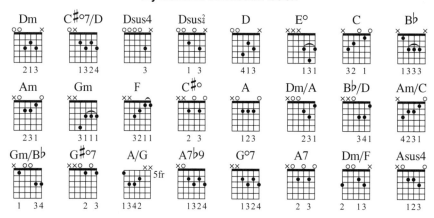

Drop D tuning:
(low to high) D-A-D-G-B-E

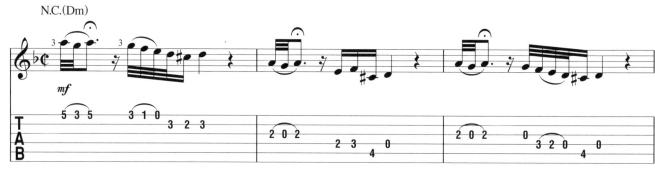

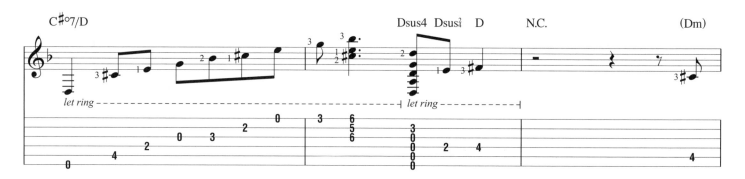

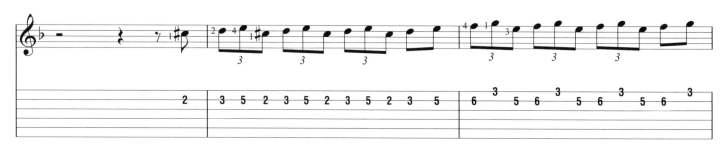

Copyright © 2015 by HAL LEONARD CORPORATION
International Copyright Secured   All Rights Reserved

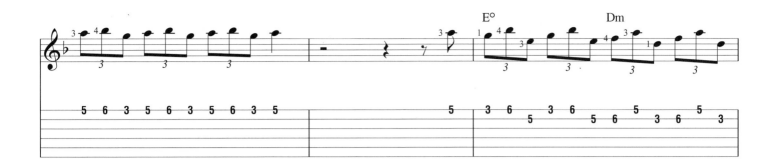

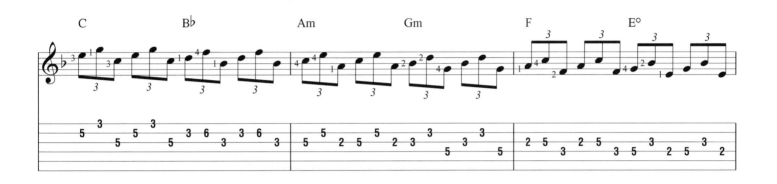

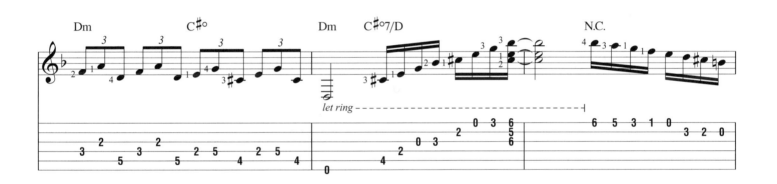

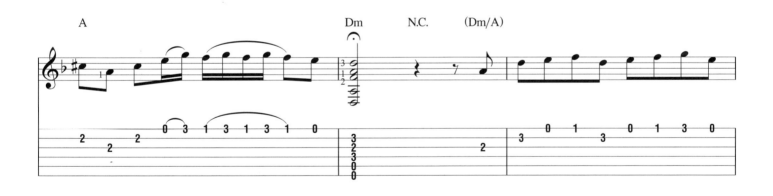

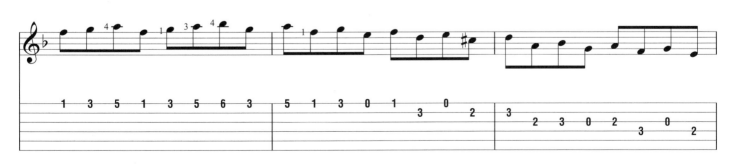

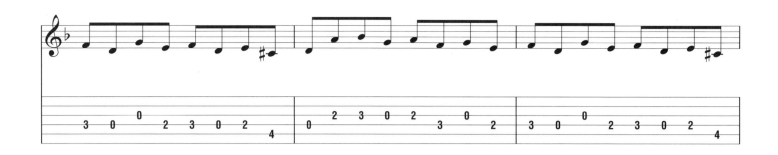

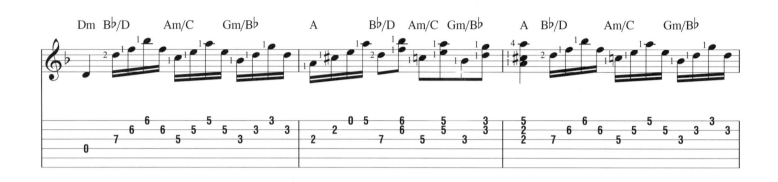

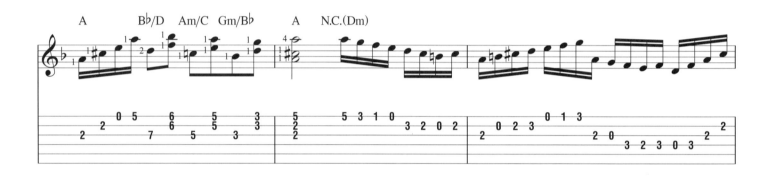

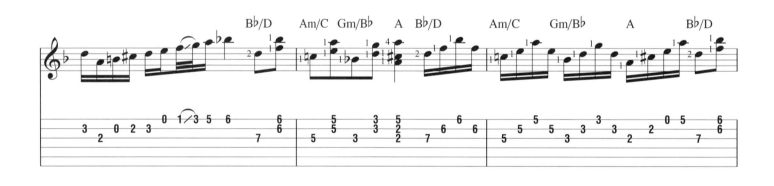

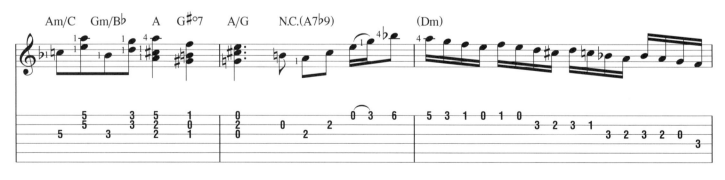

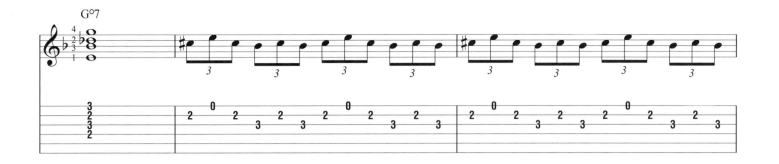

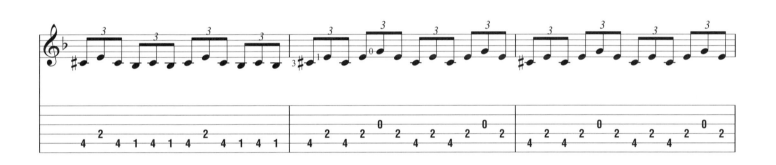
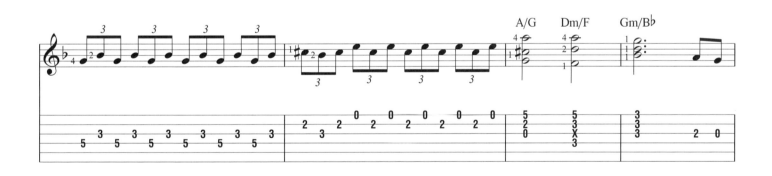
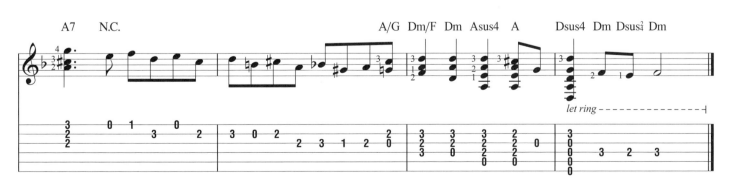

Tubular Bells

Theme from THE EXORCIST

By Mike Oldfield

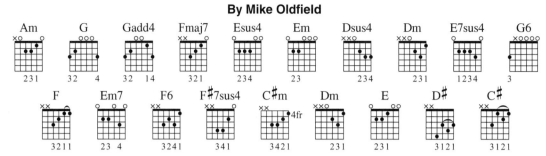

*Strum Pattern: 3

*Pick Pattern: 3

*Use Pattern 7 for ¾ meas.

**Bass arr. for gtr., next 4 meas.

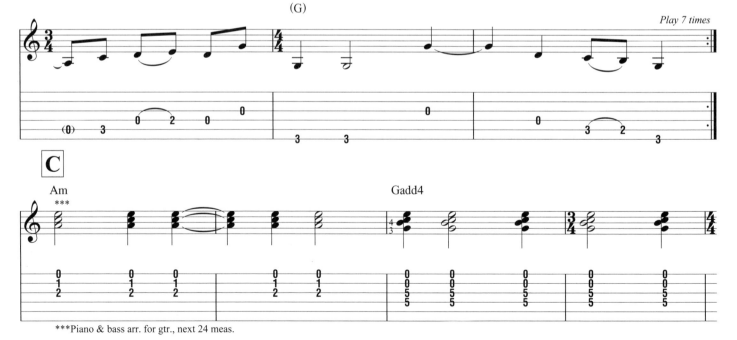

***Piano & bass arr. for gtr., next 24 meas.

Copyright © 1973 Stage Three Music (Catalogues) Limited
Copyright Renewed
All Rights Administered by BMG Rights Management (US) LLC
All Rights Reserved   Used by Permission

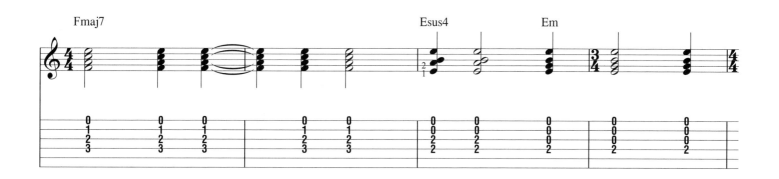

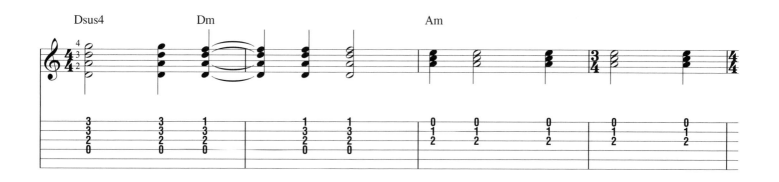

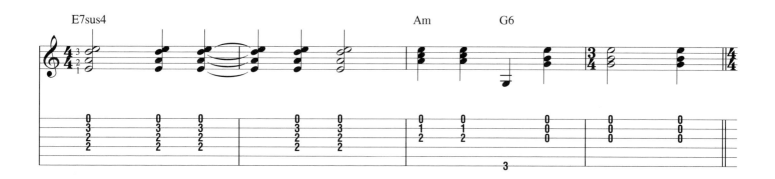

D

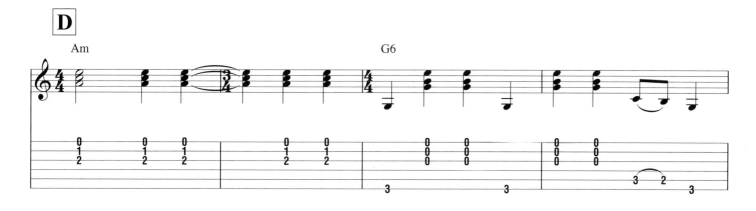

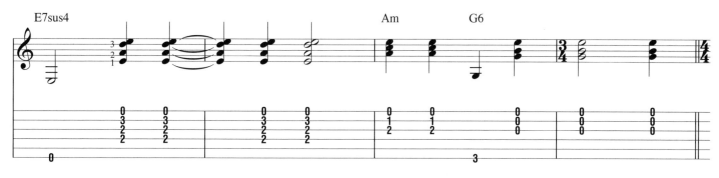

E

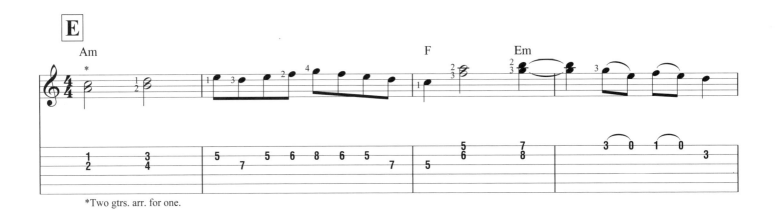

*Two gtrs. arr. for one.

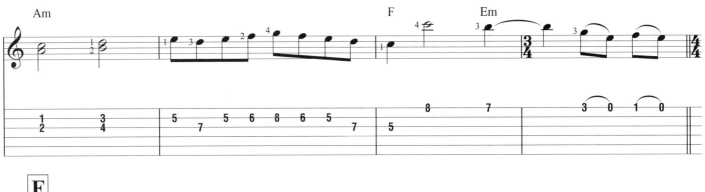

F

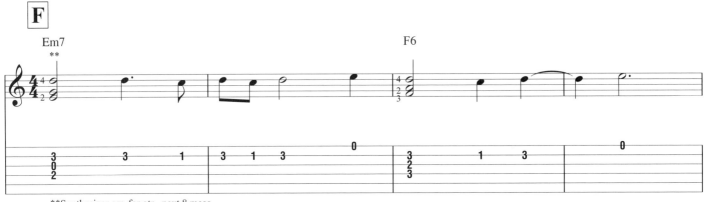

**Synthesizer arr. for gtr., next 8 meas.

G

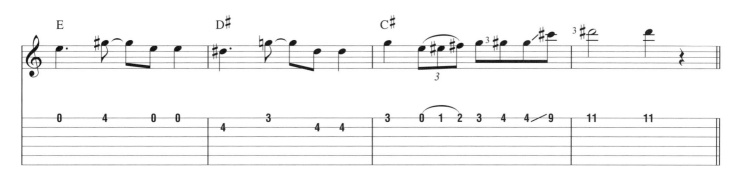

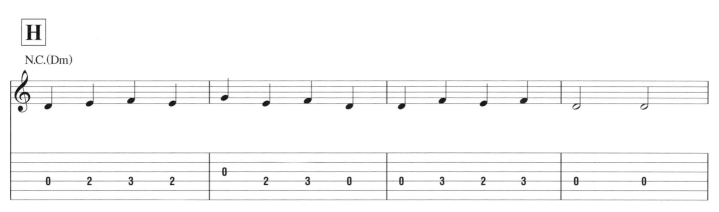

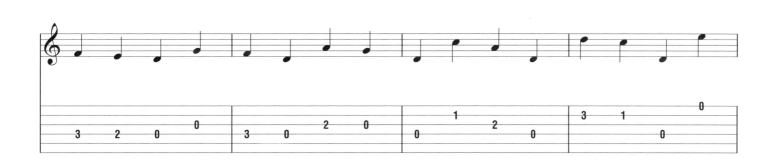

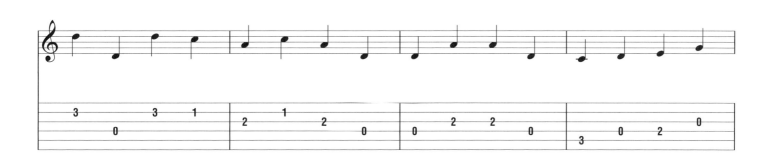

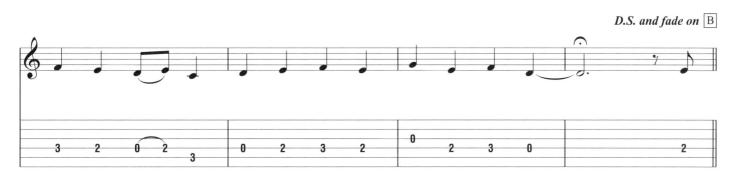

Twilight Zone Main Title

from the Television Series
By Marius Constant

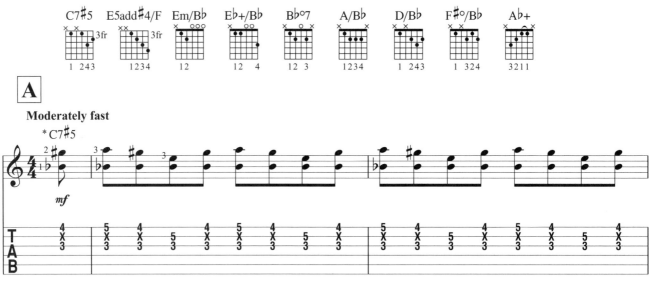

A

Moderately fast

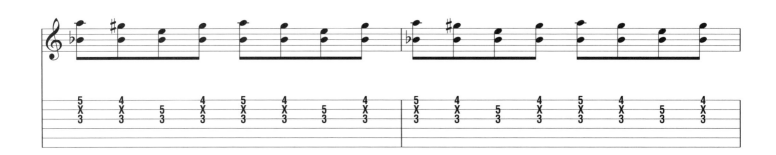

*Chord symbols reflect overall harmony.

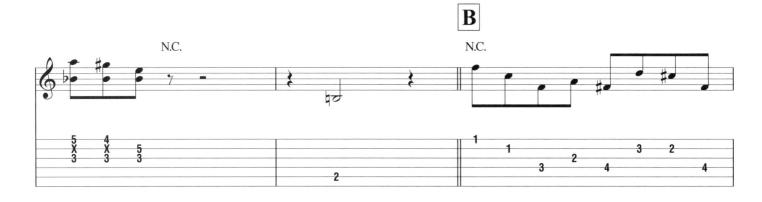

B

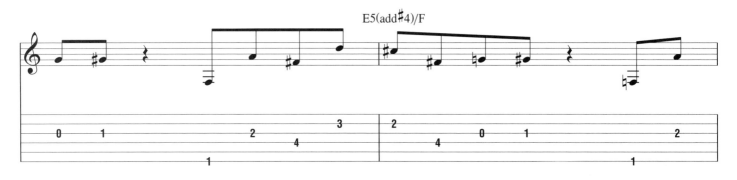

Copyright © 1960 Aspenfair Music Inc.
Copyright Renewed
All Rights Administered by Sony/ATV Music Publishing LLC, 424 Church Street, Suite 1200, Nashville, TN 37219
International Copyright Secured   All Rights Reserved

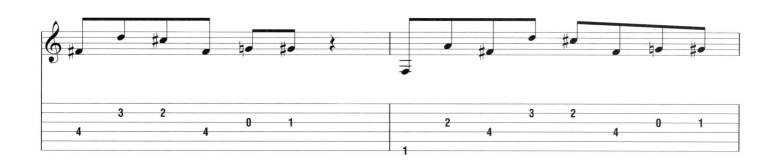

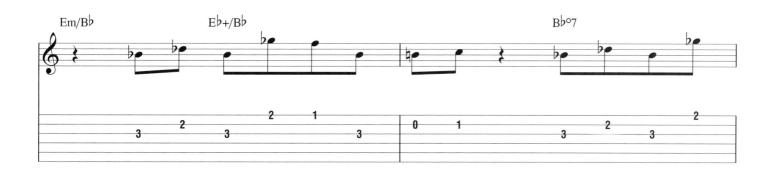

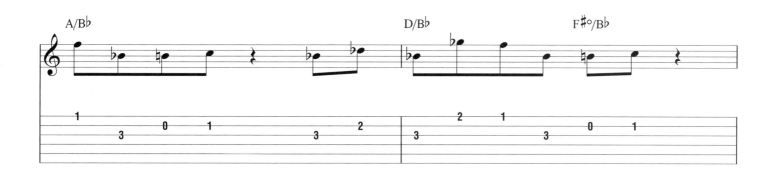

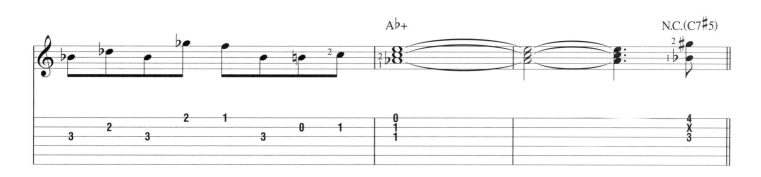

C

Welcome to My Nightmare

Words and Music by Alice Cooper and Richard Wagner

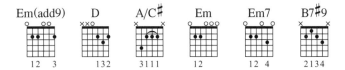

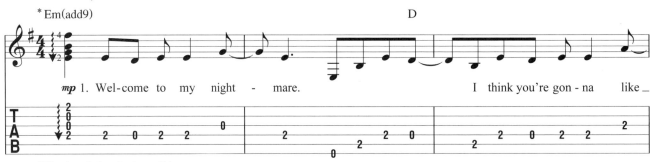

Strum Pattern: 5
Pick Pattern: 1

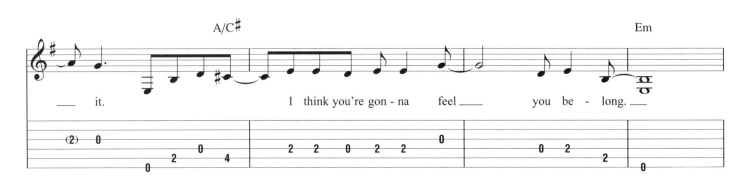

*Chord symbols reflect overall harmony.

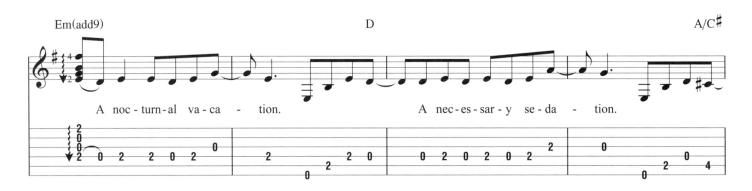

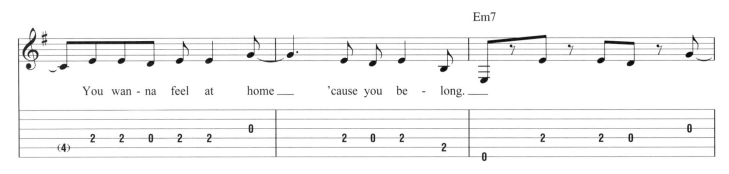

Copyright © 1975 Sony/ATV Music Publishing LLC, Ezra Music and Spirit Catalog Holdings, S.á.r.l.
Copyright Renewed
All Rights on behalf of Sony/ATV Music Publishing LLC and Ezra Music Administered by
Sony/ATV Music Publishing LLC, 424 Church Street, Suite 1200, Nashville, TN 37219
All Rights on behalf of Spirit Catalog Holdings, S.á.r.l. Controlled and Administered by Spirit One Music
International Copyright Secured   All Rights Reserved

Wel come to my night - mare, oh. _____

Verse

2. Wel-come to my break-

- down. I hope I did - n't scare ____ you.

That's just the way we are ____ when we come down. ____

We sweat and laugh and scream ____ here

Interlude

Verse

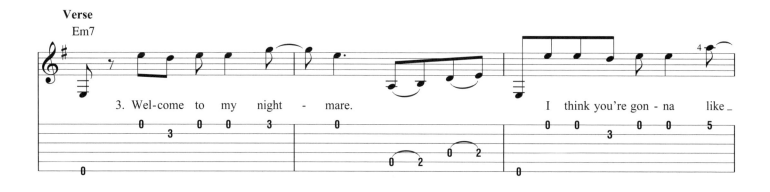

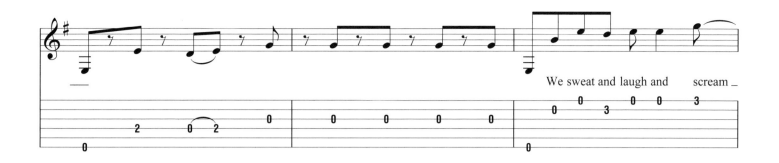

We sweat and laugh and scream

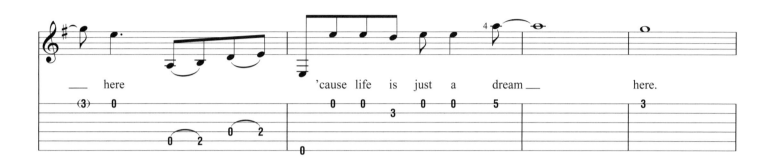

here   'cause life is just a   dream   here.

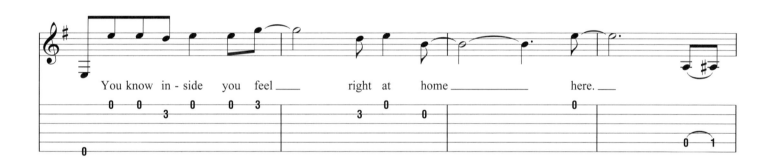

You know in - side you feel   right at home   here.

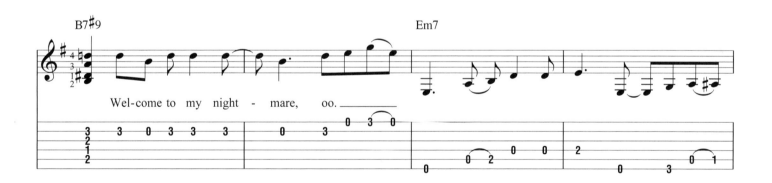

B7#9   Em7

Wel - come to my night - mare,   oo.

B7#9   N.C.   **Outro**   *Repeat and fade*
                                              Em7

Wel - come to my   break - down.

Theme from The X-Files

from the Twentieth Century Fox Television Series THE X-FILES

By Mark Snow

Strum Pattern: 3
Pick Pattern: 1

Moderately

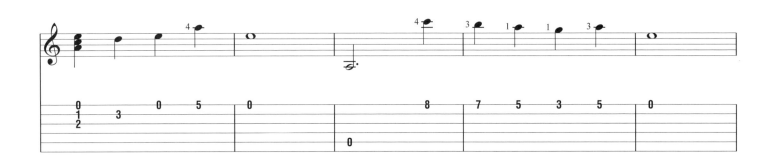

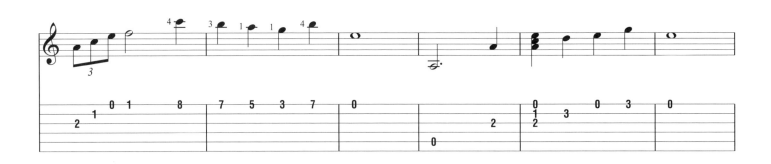

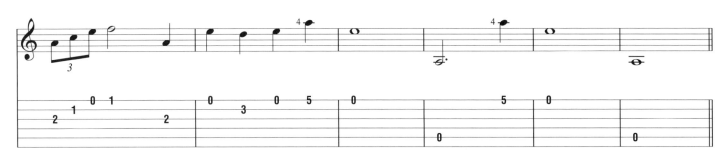

Copyright © 1993, 1995 T C F Music Publishing, Inc.
All Rights Reserved   Used by Permission

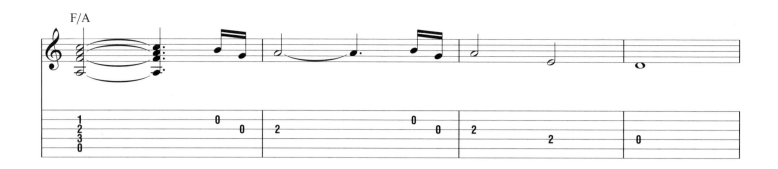

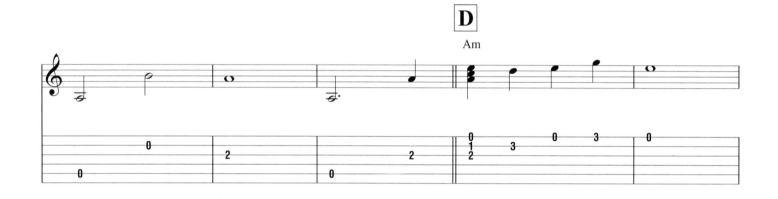

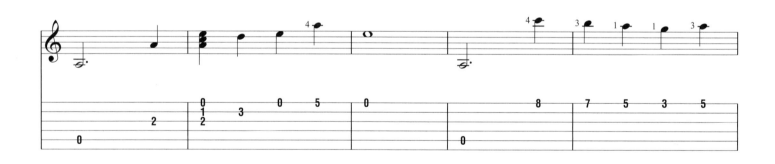

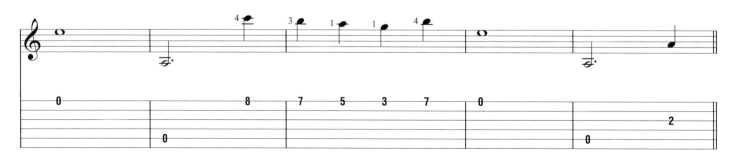

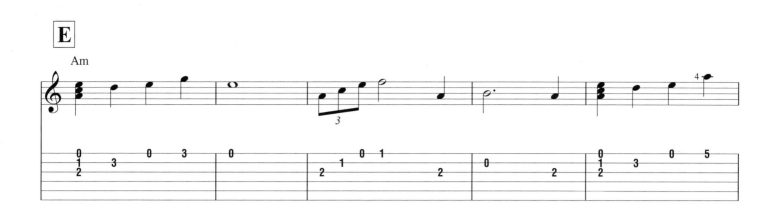

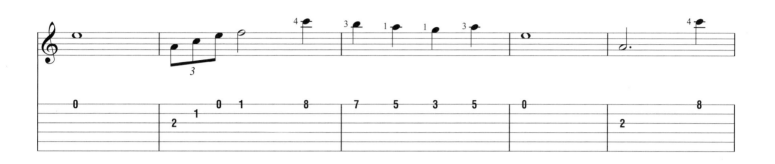

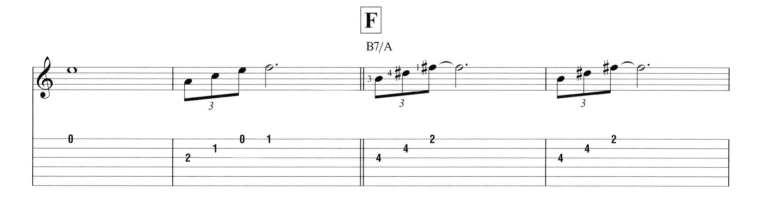

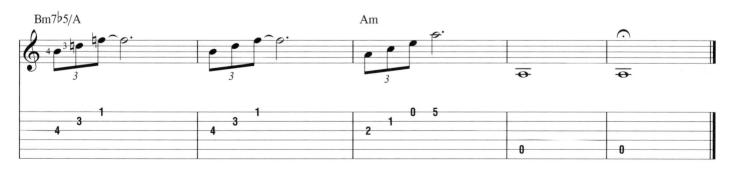

Werewolves of London

Words and Music by Warren Zevon, Waddy Wachtel and Leroy Marinell

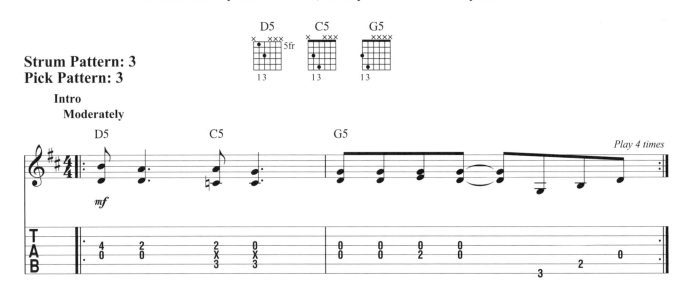

Strum Pattern: 3
Pick Pattern: 3

Intro
Moderately

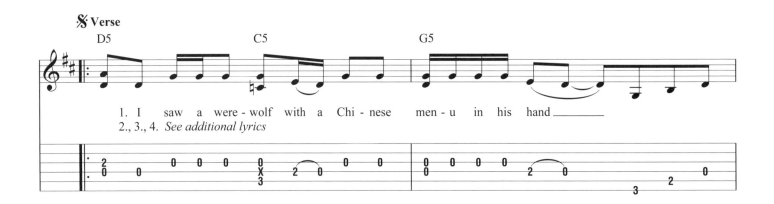

1. I saw a were - wolf with a Chi - nese men - u in his hand
2., 3., 4. *See additional lyrics*

walk - ing through the streets of So - ho in the rain.

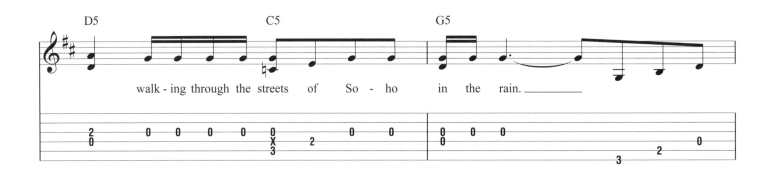

He was look - ing for the place called Lee Ho Fooks

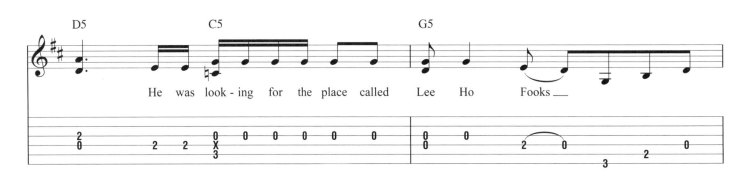

Copyright © 1978 ZEVON MUSIC, LEADSHEET LAND MUSIC and TINY TUNES
All Rights for ZEVON MUSIC Administered by SONGS OF UNIVERSAL, INC.
All Rights Reserved   Used by Permission

⊕ Coda

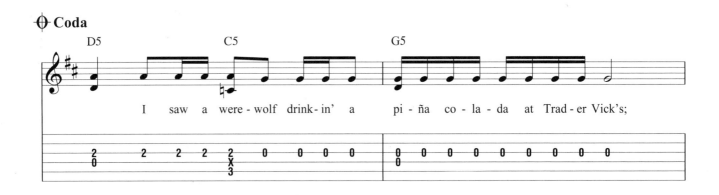

I saw a were-wolf drink-in' a pi - ña co - la - da at Trad - er Vick's;

Outro-Chorus

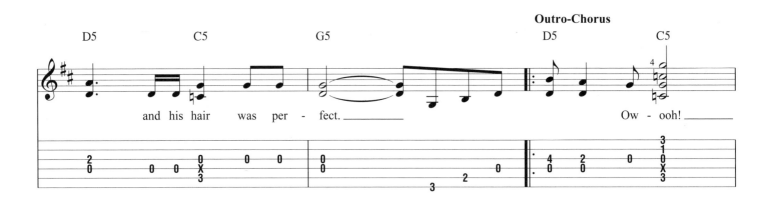

and his hair was per - fect._____ Ow - ooh!_____

Repeat and fade

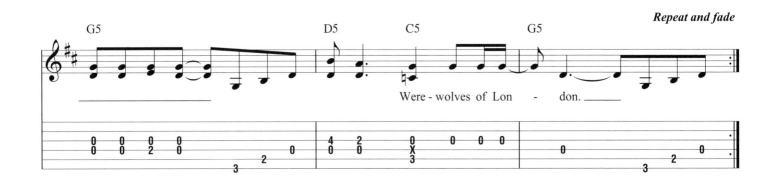

_____ Were - wolves of Lon - don._____

Additional Lyrics

2. You hear him howlin' around your kitchen door.
   You better not let him in!
   Little old lady got mutilated late last night;
   Werewolves of London again.

3. He's the hairy-handed gent who ran amuck in Kent;
   Lately, he's been overheard in Mayfair.
   You better stay away from him! He'll rip your lungs out, Jim!
   Huh! I'd like to meet his tailor.

4. Well, I saw Lon Chaney walking with the Queen,
   Doin' the werewolves of London.
   I saw Lon Chaney Junior walking with the Queen,
   Doin' the werewolves of London.
   I saw a werewolf drinkin' a piña colada at Trader Vick's;
   And his hair was perfect.